Iris Gattegno Tarbuk

SOUL MATES
How to Find and Keep True Love

2014

COPYRIGHT PAGE

Title: **SOUL MATES: How to Find and Keep True Love**
Author: **Iris Gattegno Tarbuk**
in collaboration with **Snježana Ivic**
ISBN 978-953-57179-5-9

Editor: **Mladen Gerovac**
Translation from Croatian into English: **Asenka Kramer**
Cover illustration: **Petra V. Rundek**

Name of the original: **SRODNE DUSE: Kako naci i zadrzati pravu ljubav**
First edition was published in Croatia in 2013 by Geromar d.o.o.
ISBN 978-953-57179-2-8

Copyright© Geromar d.o.o. 2013 All rights reserved.

No part of this book may be used or reproduced in any manner whatsoever, or stored in a retrieval system or transmitted by any means.

For information contact Geromar d.o.o., Zdenci 3/1, 10437 Bestovje, CROATIA
Phone: + 385 1 33 84 766
E-mail: geromar.office@gmail.com
Web site: www.dobarzivot.net

Follow Iris Gattegno Tarbuk on official Facebook page:
http://alturl.com/o832i

Library GOOD LIFE
www.dobarzivot.net
2014

CONTENTS

Foreword

INTRODUCTION

Chapter 1: WHAT IS TRUE LOVE?

Chapter 2: LOVE BETWEEN SOUL MATES

Chapter 3: LOVE AND SEX

Chapter 4: SPIRITUALITY OF THE WOMAN AND THE MAN

Chapter 5: CONTACT WITH THE SOUL OF YOUR LOVED ONE WHO DIED

Chapter 6: ATTRACTING THE SOUL MATE

Chapter 7: ADVICE FOR WOMEN AFTER FORTY

Chapter 8: SUSTAINING LOVE IN A RELATIONSHIP AND MARRIAGE

Chapter 9: SPECIAL ADVICE FOR MEN

Chapter 10: HOMOSEXUAL LOVE

Afterword

About the author

In finem

Acknowledgements

I can't express enough thanks to my husband Branimir, who has always supported me,

to my son Darel, who has taught me how to love unconditionally,

to my daughter Coral, who has also, in her own special way, taught me what unconditional love is,

to my mother Lucy, who has always put trust in me and who has taught me that dreams can become reality,

to my deceased father Moshe, who is my angel above,

to my beautiful spiritual sister Lilach and to my wonderful brother Gabriel.

I would also like to thank Snježana Ivić, who helped me write this book and to all my magnificent friends in Croatia, who love me and who accept me for who I am. Thanks to the beautiful country Croatia, which accepted me open-heartedly, with much love.

I want to express gratitude for love and the ability to love and be loved.

Iris Gattegno Tarbuk

Song of Love

*In my solitary nights
In painful longing
I'm calling you
my mystical love.*

*In magical nights
When the moon is full and bright
I'm feeling you
My mystical love.*

*You can see but cannot be seen
my nameless love.
When shall we join,
When shall we touch?*

*My lover from another world
Seek me.
Don't give up.
Give me a hand
Through the fog.
Enlighten me
My lover from another world.*

Iris Gattegno Tarbuk

Foreword

For the first time in the book form, Iris Gattegno Tarbuk, the well-known spiritual medium and guide, shares her unique insights into love: how to achieve, recognize, enjoy and how to keep it. Iris speaks about the spiritual nature of love between a man and a woman. The love which only a medium can see both in the known and the other world, in the eternal journey of searching for and finding soul mates. She speaks of happy and unhappy, long and short destinies and contacts of lovers and their carnal union with energies exchange through sex, which is the most powerful magic existing in the universe.

This book is "food for the soul", inspirational and meditative reading, and a manual with concrete advice, too. To the unloved, lonely, left, and to those deprived of their loved partner by death, Iris gives instructions, prayers and meditations how to cleanse their hearts and find their true love, how to remain in the relationship. To the couples who love each other, she gives advice how to cherish and nourish their love, how to keep their relationship happy.

Speaking about love, Iris primarily discriminates between true love and love delusions. True love joins soul mates and brings them life happiness, while love delusions result in misery, sadness, distress, disappointed people, destroyed families and unhappy children. When she talks about adultery and forgiveness, about marriage triangles and other temptations in love, she overcomes moralizing, politicizing and debating resulting from different perspectives. This book primarily aims at helping all people to find their true love – regardless of their world view, religious persuasion, sexual orientation, sex, age, appearance, health, nationality...

Love is not governed by the rational, it is not understood by scientific methods which do not detect, prove, nor do they define love. The same as God cannot be defined. Love is the part of the spirit and soul, it is born and lives in the heart. If we search for the answer to what is love, poets, prophets, psychics and many priests are closer to giving it. These are all the people who are given the gift and ability to see deeper and farther, to get insight into the otherworld. Ancient medicine men and shamans, people who healed and divined the future, also belong here. In ancient times and societies they were celebrated and worshiped, in middle ages they were prosecuted and burned at the stake, just like artists and scientists who knew more and could see deeper. With the development of science, especially quantum physics, today we more often accept them as authentic and special.

Where is the source of power and insight of psychic people? Where do they search for and find answers to their questions about the past, present and future? In this book the term used is *akasha* from the ancient Indian philosophy, from old Vedic texts and the Upanishads. It designates the space where all answers to all crucial questions about the world and the man reside, starting with where we are coming from and where we are going.

Akasha can be described as the otherworld life spirit and spiritual power, as an indestructible source of omnipotence, all knowledge, as a space filled with the substance from which everything starts and where everything ends. *Akasha* is a universal, omnipresent and an all-inclusive soul from which everything that exists has been created. It is an impregnating existence. Everything was created from *akasha*: substance, energy, gravity and all laws of nature, memory, mental creations which we experience as innovations, discoveries and inventions.

Among the famous historical persons, prophet Nostradamus, inventor Nikola Tesla and philosopher Rudolf Steiner had an insight into *akasha*. Rudolf Steiner, Austrian philosopher, esotericist and the founder of anthroposophy, as a general knowledge about the spiritual nature and interconnectedness of the world, universe and the man (born in Croatian Međimurje, Donji Kraljevec), insightfully established revolutionary rules of biodynamic agriculture prevailing in ecological agriculture nowadays, although he never practiced it himself. He also brought new knowledge to medicine and art, although he was neither a physician, nor an artist. Steiner claimed that *akasha* was a recording at the mental level where all past and future were kept, where all events at the material level, not only at our planet, but in the whole universe were recorded. Exactly from these recordings, Steiner figured out the postulates which are today widely accepted and used in the practice of biodynamic agriculture and in Waldorf schools and kindergartens.

Ingenious inventor Nikola Tesla, in his unpublished work "Man's Greatest Achievement" wrote about the primary substance filling all space. Tesla compared this primary substance with *akasha*. By that he explained his ingenious inventions, because the primary substance (*akasha*) was a sort of force field turning into substance under the influence of cosmic energy. When the influence ceases to exist, the substance ceases to exist and is back in *akasha*. Tesla had so precise visions that he saw machines and his other inventions in detail to later draft, patent and operate them in reality, based on his insights.

Who else can have an insight in *akasha*, if s/he is not a genius, scientist, inventor. Indeed, *akasha* is directly available primarily to the people especially endowed from their birth. However, through history and practice it has been shown that actually all people are born with a potential to enter *akasha* and reach its content. This requires some special personality characteristics and above all – persistent practicing. More than all it takes total relaxation with the ability of a strong focus, openness of the mind and the heart and a strong desire to explore the unknown. On top of these premises, the access to *akasha* requires steady meditation, cleansing the heart and the soul...

Accessing the *akashic* records, we can, in the otherworld, approach other persons as other persons can approach us and our personal records. Indeed, this kind of universe internet enables us to find a soul mate with whom we can develop true love. Readings of Iris Gattegno Tarbuk – the author of this book of help and self-help are directed at exactly that part of *akasha*.

In her sources of knowledge and considerations she uses the *third eye*. What is it about? The *third eye* is the focus of the oriental mystical meditation, it is placed in the middle of the forehead, above eyes, and everybody has it. In ordinary people it is incipient, while in the gifted, it is very active. It can be used to see the *aura*, the energy of each human, while the Tibetan lamas and Indian yogi interpret that the *third eye* enables one to "*be at two places at the same time, walk on water, levitate, travel through time and space...*"

Back to the central theme of this book – the concept of love. Love is perfect both in its content and form, it does not allow for any calculations and limitations.

Otherwise it is not perfect, nor is it true. Love is something ideal, pure, without reservation, complete. If a relationship of two people is not like this, then it is not true love. In everyday life we name many relationships between two people 'love', although they are far from the concept of ideal love. That concept, besides the perfection of the soul, inevitably involves the body, so a human being is limited by that physicality. Is it possible to attain such a balance of the spirit and the body so as to achieve true love?

Iris Gattegno Tarbuk, a spiritual medium, a *soul reader*, a person who can see deeper and farther, who is close to the otherworld, shows that the ideal of genuine, true love can be achieved by everybody.

Through pages of this book, she communicates her spiritual insights to her readers and develops her spiritual experience giving concrete instructions how to attract the person with whom such love is possible, how to meet one's soul mate.

In this book, Iris answers two key questions about happiness in life: how to find love and how to keep it.

Mladen Gerovac
Editor

INTRODUCTION

Dear readers,

With this book, I want to introduce you into the world of love. Although it is about my spiritual interpretations and experience, regardless of how much you may be disposed to these, through simple and clear explanations, you will be able to recognize your lives, your happy or unhappy love, your mistakes and delusions. Besides practical advice, prayers and meditations, I am offering ways how each one of you can cleanse your heart and eliminate interferences, obstacles, obstructions and barriers which prevent you from loving and being loved. I want to open passages to that state of your soul in which you will enjoy life with your soul mate, in which you will find that person (some of you more of them) with whom you will feel complete, fulfilled, happy and loved.

Reading souls

As early as a young girl I started spontaneously discovering my gift of reading souls. Through my puzzled child eyes I watched men and women around me who were seriously suffering due to the lack of love and attention. Their souls desperately sought love, craving it, they would have done anything to find it, to experience it... but they didn't know how to reach it, how to realize it. Love would generally remain only suffering and pining, merely a distant, unrequited desire.

Later, growing up, developing into a woman who also experienced love, I reached a deeper knowledge. I gradually became aware that the main reason of that human deep love disaster and misery is that the majority of people seek and desperately need love, while at the same time they don't know what love is – don't know how to love unconditionally and how to receive such love. And when they start thinking that they have finally found it, and when after some shorter or longer time that happiness is there no more, they are disappointed understanding that it was not love at all, but a delusion to which they easily abandoned themselves.

After such disappointments some women and men become so bitter as to completely give up on love – they wither, yield to depression, their heart petrifies, they stop hoping, loving, living. The more persistent ones start searching. And in that *searching – finding – short-lived rapture – breaking up* of the relationship which, in their delusion they consider to be love, there is a lot of tears, stress, unhappiness, conflicts, suffering, disappointment, sometimes even illness, or worse, giving up on life.

Level of the heart

Why most people fail at finding love? I asked for an answer to this question in meditation, in the eternal source of universal knowledge, in *akasha*. Where do we make mistakes? I started receiving messages that the majority seek love from the low, physical level, from the position of their need for energy food in this way: *I need love, I am hungry for love, I must get that food, I must feast upon...* And they satisfy their need in the sexual intercourse, exchanging energy at the level of the lower abdomen. Then they are unhappy and hungry and again they start their search for food. Their hunger can be satiated only by true love which comes from the spiritual level, from the level of the heart.

It can be visually represented like this: each of us carries one small light in our hearts. Something like a votive candle which is sometimes lit and sometimes not. In some people that light is stronger, in others, it is weaker. In some of us it can become as strong as a lighthouse. The more the person is enlightened, aware, the purer his/her heart is, the more the person works on her/himself, the more the person helps others, that person's light is stronger and may attract soul mates. Among the attracted people there will also be the one with whom the person will build true love, fulfillment, harmony, happiness.

Salvific light

How does the light carried in our heart affect others? Life is sometimes so difficult that it seems we are held in captivity in a cold, dark tunnel in which everything around us is permeated with cold, impenetrable darkness. When we see a light dot, we will immediately rush to that liberation from the darkness suffocating us. Now we are two light dots. One light feeds the other and together we shine stronger. From the deep darkness we attract the third light, then the fourth, the fifth...

Indeed, we, people, feed each other with the light from our hearts, so even those who do not have the light will come to feed on others' lights. They will feel that there is something different and better in us, and they will try to awake it in themselves.

Cleansing and awakening

As a spiritual medium and guide, I have been on the mission of helping people for three decades now. During the past six years I have been running workshops in Zagreb, the capital of Croatia, where I help men and women looking for partners. I help them cleanse and awaken their hearts so that they can fill them with light to attract soul mates and true love into their lives. Cleansing and awakening the heart in the guided joint meditation in the workshops proved to be much more successful than I dared hope when I started with them. The majority of candidates with so awakened hearts started experiencing strange things. I use the word strange because when love entered their lives it was not even close to how they planned it, because love always goes through totally different passages.

SMS from the distant past

Thus one of my friends, exactly at the moment when together with others in the group lay relaxed and in meditation with her eyes closed, she was opening the door of the miraculous garden with the temple in which she would cleanse her heart, received an SMS message sent by a dear person from the distant past. It was an invitation to meet again. "Does it make sense to waste time on something that vanished a long time ago?", she was reluctant at first. However, her curiosity prevailed and she went to the meeting enticed by the fact that the message arrived exactly when she was meditating in the workshop for attracting a soul mate. "Is it possible that the process has already started, that powers of the universe already work for me? Is it the sign that he is the one?", her questions swarmed.

So the two of them met and what happened is exactly what would be unimaginable for her only a few days before. A new flame of love kindled out of the long dead ashes. My friend thus finally found happiness in that real, intense love which she so strongly desired.

Miraculous encounter in the air

It also "worked" for a very unhappy and lonely business woman leading a successful company where she did her managerial job wonderfully. Unfortunately, her career success was not followed by happiness in love. Although in her late thirties, she was gradually losing all hope that her wish might be granted, that her life might be complete, that she could have that too... She decided to do the last thing – from Split, where she lived, she came to the workshop *soul mates* in Zagreb. Her wish was granted at the very return home. High above the clouds, during only half an hour flight to Split, she experienced the karmic meeting. She met her soul mate, the person who will be the man of her life. They *accidentally* had tickets next to each other. With this man from the airplane, the successful manager has children and happy marriage today.

Never give up

I often joyfully remember a very dear lady in her golden age who joined meditations to cleanse her heart, not even thinking about some love relationship, but wishing to achieve better harmony in life. What happened was that after a couple of days she met an almost forgotten man from her student days (whom she last saw at the college) and that they fell in love anew.

Hence, no matter how disappointed and broken you may be, don't give up your quest for happiness and love. Work on yourself every day and love will come. Life is hard, but when you live it close to your soul mate, then everything is good, everything is right and everything is beautiful. The lucky ones among us are surrounded by many soul mates. It may be your child, parents and friends with whom you have a special, very close relationship. However, if you are not that lucky, if you don't live with your soul mates, don't have soul mates among your friends, don't work with soul mates, you will always sense a lingering, undefined, little dull feeling that you are missing something crucial in order to be complete.

Becoming better, you fare better

In the contemporary stressful, fast and superficial world, few people know how to live spiritually, and the primordial holy energy possessed once by women, who by the help of that energy ruled over nature, is almost destroyed. Little of that holy energy that remained is so deeply suppressed in us that we are not even aware of it, and we certainly don't know how to rein nor how to activate it.

That alienation from our primordial nature and a lack of spirituality are the main reasons why many people lead constantly unhappy lives. That misery with which we excruciatingly tumble over day after day, go to sleep unhappy, wake up to the new morning even more unhappy, is by some people considered inevitable, something which has to be accepted.

"That is life and nothing can be done about that. It has to be so. There is no better way."

So they consent to the sordidly low level of living and energy, consent to the "valley of tears".

Others are aware that something is not as it should be and search for ways of improvement. They work on themselves, improve and say:

"It is difficult for us and we all have problems, but let us work on them.

Let us resolve them. We can always do something."

Results are always there: the better people become, the better they fare.

Love forever

On that path of quest, working on yourself, cleansing and awakening your heart, you will meet your soul mate, too. It is that person with whom you don't need any special conversations, nor explanations.

It is that person who is your home, the one with whom you feel fulfilled even when there are arguments and conflicts between you, even when you aren't together. Even when one of you leaves this world, when s/he dies, your souls are still connected by the love you feel, and deep down you know that you will meet and be together again...

Iris Gattegno Tarbuk

Chapter 1

WHAT IS TRUE LOVE?

When love is real, you don't ask anything from your partner.
If s/he loves you, you have everything you desire.
You ask for nothing and have everything.
That is true love.

Philosophers, theologians, scientists and wise men of all sorts, from the East and from the West, since the beginning of time have devoted much time, attention, systematic research, speeches and written pages to discerning the essence of love, searching for the answer to the question: what is love? They have been searching for its source, scope and meaning. They have been trying to analyze it, demystify, explain... in their huge desire to assess, define and simplify it, to make it available and simply put, in terms of the modern consumer society, to make it more "user friendly", to wrap it up into a *ready-to-go* pill.

Despite their devotion and endeavors they haven't found the formula of knowing the essence of love, because they can only explain by definitions. Love is infinite and as such it cannot be defined.

Love is an act, and emotion, and hunch, and hope, and faith, and basic need, and meaning, and the purpose of existence and eternal energy in the universe. It dwells in all dimensions. Love has created everything that is created. Love is God, and when we love, we become a part of that perfection. This is why we all so desperately want love, we want to love and be loved.

This is why it is important to understand that love can be experienced only through the heart. It doesn't live in the rational. Reason cannot discern it, neither can the brain rein it. Love emerges from other human cores – from the heart and soul. Reason is more often in conflict with these, than in unity.

When in your heart you experience true love, that love which has no limits in time nor in space, you will know... And never again will you be the same, because you have joined the strongest power in the universe – that eternal energy that has created everything.

How universal the wish to get answers about love is, can be shown by statistics on internet browsers, where among the most often asked questions in all countries of the world are "what is love" and "how to love". It is very sad that today, while sophisticated machines we designed are searching for other forms of life in the universe, here, on planet Earth, we are still uncertain about answers to basic human questions about love.

The majority of us cannot recognize, develop, sustain, nourish, show, give, receive love... and the lack of love is one of the most frequent causes why people violently and even cruelly deprive other people, and even themselves of life.

Love is a very broad idea including various kinds of love, from the love which connects God, the creator with everything he has created, to our love for friends, parents, the child, the partner, ourselves, job, nature, country...

Love eliminates the feeling of separation between us and the other, thus we express our love for God by feeling one with all beings and the universe he has created. Love between a man and a woman, romantic or partner love with which we are dealing in this book, symbolically reminds us of the need to return to the unity with everything created, the unity of divine male and divine female principles as the principles of creation itself.

Or, as the great philosopher and poet Rumi said:

I am not I, you are not you, you are not I.
I am I, you are you, and you are I.
We have joined together,
and no more do I know: am I you, or are you I?

Therefore I won't try to define love. It is easier to say what love is not, than to express everything that love is.

Love is not a magic wand granting wishes

There is that delusion that love is like a magic wand which will, only if you somehow get hold of it, grant you everything you wish, happiness, wealth, a state of bliss and a *good and happy life forever.* This collective myth is especially supported by romantic stories and Hollywood movies where it is always self-understood that after a passionate kiss spiced with words "I love you. I will always love you." and a marriage, always follows a *happy end*, or *lived happily ever after*, without everyday problems.

That is why the woman often sees her "lived happily ever after" like this:

I want to have a beautiful body, I want to have magnificent hair,
I want to have a handsome and rich husband. He will
buy me a beautiful car, I will have a lot of money, I will have
cute children, beautiful house and clothes...

The average man has similar expectations:

I want to have a beautiful body, to be strong, muscular and athletic, I want to be rich, to have a good car, I want a pretty wife. She will love me, give birth to beautiful children and everybody will envy us...

Almost all of us make lists of various wishes and requirements and expect that through love with our ideal partner, they will be granted.

Majority of couples don't enter relationships for love, but because they need to *have* somebody or something, to *gain* something they miss, to possess something, to fill in some existential void, to get rid of boredom, powerlessness, or because of *the people,* in order to be more appreciated – because: "What will they think about me if I do not have a husband, a wife..."

Thus before anything, we need to be aware of one basic fact: when we quest for a partner with a wish list starting with *I want, I need, give me* – it is when love cannot develop, no matter how much we may fool ourselves and pledge that we *truly love*.

And quite the opposite, some people have achieved and gained what they wished for, as if they didn't desire romantic love, but only a sexual relationship, and a sporadic one, too. In recent years I have met several such couples who live in a relationship, i.e. a marriage they entered like an agreed friendly partnership, searching romance and sex with someone else in short lived adventures out of that relationship.

Not with their beloved, but with a friend, they created a home where they fulfilled their material and other needs of a stable, happy life, having children in that partnership. And that satisfies them.

Is it true love? No, but the way they achieved happiness living together is such that it suits them. Even if it is because they have given up on the quest for true love with uncertain outcome and created their safe life shelter in a friendship, we have to respect their choice.

In love, like in the way how happy life is realized, rules and regulations that could be applied to all people equally, really do not exist.

Love starts with ourselves

Love doesn't start so that at one moment, at one fatal meeting we fall in love with someone. Love starts with ourselves, with our love for ourselves, for life, for everything that has been created... Such love makes us capable of loving another person and of being loved by that person unconditionally. When love is real, you don't ask for anything from your partner. If s/he loves you, you have everything you want. So, you don't ask for anything, but you have everything you want. That is true love.

Most often it is not the case and we return to the sad truth of life that a large number of love relationships have nothing to do with true love.

Let us say you got married with the whole scenario you were dreaming of as an unforgettable introduction into the lasting life happiness. It was just like in a movie: a beautiful wedding dress, the bride like a princess, church and the wedding hall all in flowers, fateful "I do", your mother's tearful eyes, your father's proud smile, wedding rings exchanged, the first waltz, joyful wedding party guests, white tiered cake, congratulations, presents, honeymoon... Everything looks like a fairy tale, but what put the bride and the bridegroom together? True love or temporary doting and infatuation? Has all that performance been played only for a tick "achieved" under marriage, love, husband... on that wish list created by a young girl dreaming of her happy future? If the wedding was meant to fulfill a wish list starting with *I want, I need, give me,* the life will soon turn into an unplanned and unwanted, but ruthless, ugly scenario.

Marriage partner isn't a fairy machine with the purpose of granting your wishes and fulfilling your needs. When you understand that he doesn't deliver everything you want, you may start showering with the whole classical arsenal of criticism: "How do you think we can live with your small salary?", "I am wearing a crombie coat and Joe bought his wife a mink fur coat!", "Where have you been so long when your job finishes at three?" "What did you do with your friends the whole afternoon, if only I knew what it was you talked about so long..." Or he may criticize her: "This stuff you have cooked is not eatable!", "If you talked to your friends less, the flat would be cleaner, and telephone bills would be smaller!", "Who could afford all that money you can spend?"... Up to those fatal reproofs and conclusions with no return: "You ruined my life!", "You are the worst thing that happened in my life.", "Where was I looking when I met you?", "Where has that man I married disappeared?"... And the end.

It has never been love.

Love is not possessing

As early as a girl I became aware that the majority of couples weren't happy in their love, but mostly acted their happiness. They embraced each other, held hands, smiled blissfully while deep inside there was unhappiness, darkness, emptiness and desperation. Within them and between them there was no true intimacy and closeness, everything was only physical and on the surface. They held hands to show everybody that they possessed each other.

When you are in love, you think that the person belongs only to you. That person is something you want and must have and then sustain at any price. When you think you are losing him/her, you become desperate. If s/he doesn't want to be yours any more, you lose reason, go wild. You behave like a spoiled brat in a shop who doesn't want to hear mum's "no". That is the state you are in: you want, you suffer and you must have.

It is by no means love.

Today, when I can read people inside with a much stronger insight and bigger experience than I could do it as a girl, I can see unfulfilled needs, wishes, hunger, much clearer... but there is no true love. We search for it, we desire it, we argue about it, we deeply suffer, we even kill for love and in the name of love – but in most cases, it is not love at all.

We all often tend to forget that love is based in freedom. Love is not prison, although we unconditionally surrender. In such a relationship I love myself and you love yourself. I, as a whole, love you, as a whole. Than a good relationship can begin, the love which we can enjoy.

When we really love, we are in the state of harmony. We need nothing. There is no jealousy nor need to possess in true love. We are happy that our beloved exists. We enjoy the very fact like a mother loves her newly born baby: watches him/her breathing and is happy for that.

It is difficult to reach that level of a relationship that both are ready to be free, that both are ready to give their partner the freedom to be what s/he is, to go where and when s/he wants and do what s/he wants. It can be achieved when we love ourselves.

When we give ourselves everything we need, when we do not ask others to fulfill our needs, it is then that we can be free to enjoy a relationship. Then we will let our beloved enjoy his/her hobbies and friends, books, journeys, or whatever s/he enjoys, without fear that somebody or something is depriving us from his/her love.

Even if your partner is cheating and it hurts you, become aware of the moment, of that feeling. Ask yourself honestly why it really hurts. Is it because somebody took something that belongs to you? Is it because that man or that woman is your property? Is s/he not with you because s/he really wants it?

Each of us, every man and every woman is a person in himself or herself, with his or her own soul and body, with his or her own energy and needs. The truth is that people rarely accept this in a partner relationship because we have an image of our relationship like this:

I chose him. I love him.
He loves me. He is mine.
When everything around me is as I want it,
I will be happy.

That is not love.

Jealousy isn't a part of love

If you love, don't be jealous of every step s/he makes. Even if s/he is cheating on you, there is a reason why s/he is passing through that life experience... Discover what it is in you that made you choose exactly that partner and created exactly such a relationship. Try to use it for your further spiritual growth, and as in the old saying, don't let it break you, make it strengthen you.

When you once understand what balance you have in yourself, what your partner's cheating is warning you of, you have almost overcome some limitation of yours which pushed you – of course, totally unconsciously – into arranging just a situation like that in the movie of your life.

Each partner has the right to a free choice and that choice is indubitable. This does not imply that I am promoting adultery. I only state that true love, genuine love dance, can develop only based on mutual freedom, and under no circumstances ever in a relationship where a partner is property.

Love dance is such that when one partner steps forward, the other, in the same rhythm, joyfully and naturally steps backward; when the other steps forward, the one equally naturally and joyfully steps backward. Only when you achieve that your relationship is such a harmonious dance, and not a battle where partners fight for domination – you are on the right path.

I openly admit that this is hard to achieve for everybody, and for me, too, but it is certainly the ideal we need to strive for because true love doesn't come from our egos, but from our souls. Our ego wants to keep, possess, have only for ourselves, dominate over the other... Jealousy, which can be devastating, even life threatening, comes from the ego, while true love brings only pleasure and joy, not suffering.

Therefore, from the moment you become jealous in a relationship, miserable and nervous, be aware of the indisputable fact that it isn't an expression of love and either get out of the relationship or try to develop love so that you give your partner freedom.

Because of all the painful experience happening to other couples, many, especially men, feel fear of love. They avoid longer relationships, especially a marriage, like a deadly trap, as if it were some sticky spider web into which they would be entangled like flies and become helpless, and then their partner would, like a hungry spider, feed on them their whole life, take away their freedom, deprive them from all pleasures and eventually suck out their very life.

In most human relationships, and in partner relationships, too, one partner is stronger and dominates. I see that even in childhood loves, but it doesn't work in love.

For example, when the woman is strong, she gives the man signals about what she loves and what she wants. If he is in love, he will fulfill all her wishes, but after some time, he will start feeling he has had enough. He will feel fed up with serving her, fulfilling all her whims and fads, and when he tries to change something, do something to his liking, when he stops satisfying her wishes, she will go mad. She won't allow that, she will try to put things in order. There won't be much happiness in the relationship after that.

If the woman forgets that the man has a life even without her, he feels such a big pressure that he tries to drift away, to cheat on her, to go to pubs in male company, into football or various typically male hobbies like hunting or similar. Some men remain silent and do their stuff, while others demonstratively just go and come home later and later because they are unhappy, trying to run away and save themselves. In both cases the most frequent result is that the husband and the wife get in conflict, hurt each other and divorce.

There are indeed men with whom such a possessive wife's behaviour agrees, some return to their childhood in such relationships because their wife's behaviour reminds them of their mother, even to a degree where it enters the psychiatric domain.

I could exemplify the above mentioned with dominant men, too. Although it isn't my aim to take sides with one sex, I could see in my counseling with couples that such possessiveness in a relationship is most often the problem women have.

Give your partner freedom, because:

When you love somebody and s/he loves you,

then you trust each other and you are happy.

Give him/her freedom including that final test of infinite and unconditional love when you are happy if the loved one is happy, even if it is in a relationship with someone else.

When love is coming to us

It is said that love comes alone and uninvited. In a way, that is true. When you are ready for love, you will certainly attract a partner into your life. However, does it really mean you are ready? If you want love to become a part of your life, you have to become love yourself, and you have to work on yourself to achieve that.

It often happens that love doesn't enter your life because there are various blockages in you. For example, you think you aren't beautiful enough, educated enough, young enough... All these prevent you from nurturing the inner feeling that you are worthy and deserving love and being such, you cannot attract the partner of your dreams.

If you want love, live love, be in love with life, believe that you are worthy of love and the energy with which you will then radiate will turn your dreams into reality.

To achieve that, you have to work much on yourself, remove your blockages from the past, elevate your heart frequency, get to know and start loving yourself... Sometimes you don't have to do all this because life may occasionally be a game with accidental winnings.

Don't take yourself, life, love, rigidly and too seriously, let the unplanned variances happen.

Believe that your life is already perfect and that it is remarkably leading you towards the fulfillment of your wishes.

Get free of fear and start your quest for the life play, live your love, go out, use websites to meet someone, forget the doubts about going to *blind dates*. Meet as many people as possible and you will find your soul mate among them.

Whatever happens – never give up on love

I often see that people who have been disappointed in love close their hearts. This is especially true about men and women above forty. They don't believe in love any more so they lower the criteria about a partner to the level of pure survival in two. Sometimes they are satisfied with searching for and finding any partner who is willing to live with them in order not to be alone in their old age and in sickness.

After some time they transform into cold and rigid persons, they become bitter and don't enjoy anything. As if they were living dead – they behave like zombies, with not even a bit of energy, will, wish, or feeling, and once they become such, they lose all chances for love forever. Therefore, however bitter, sad, abandoned or miserable you may be after a love breakdown, leave your heart open to love, sustain your love energy.

You may get help by listening to some song you feel expresses your emotions. Watching romantic love movies and reading love fiction may also help, the more if you have a nice cry during that (I recommend this especially to men!) Pets can also help. If you don't have any, adopt one from the animal shelter. Give them love, they will return it and thus you will sustain your love energy. I have a friend, a very spiritual person, who adopts old, handicapped and sick animals from the shelter, the ones nobody else wants. She enjoys the enormous love these grateful animals show in return.

Help someone in need.

Volunteer, devote yourself to children with special needs, to the poor, the sick, the miserable. Make their lives nicer, better, easier. It will bring light into your heart, help you sustain, live and vibrate the love energy, and then it will open the path to true love for you.

Love as a source of health

When we love, when we are balanced psychologically, mentally, spiritually and energetically, then we achieve the state of perfect health. People in the energy of love can achieve such a balanced state.

Nowadays many people with a strong love energy aren't healthy. Our way of life – exhausting, stressful and alienated is primarily responsible for that. Our air, water and food are polluted. It is clear that such a way of life needs to be changed, it is necessary to live healthy. Love energy alone followed with the modern way of life isn't sufficient for health. Besides, persons with a strong love energy take over others' troubles, they are empathetic, suffer together with others, and all that throws them out of the state of balance and of health.

I had the honor of meeting only one person with a strong love energy who helps people and their troubles don't endanger him, don't encumber and exhaust him. It is Dalai Lama whom I met during his stay in Croatia. In his company, he seems to be with you and somewhere far away at the same time. In a way, he manages to approach you, to transfer his love energy, while at the same time, the suffering and pain of the people around him don't devastate him. His balance was not shattered by the problems of people he talked with, although he empathized with them, neither did he take their problems and suffering on while giving them love and consolation. The power of his energy is such that it protects him; he is like a shiny light gleaming with such a glow that no darkness can reach him.

Chapter 2

LOVE BETWEEN SOUL MATES

*When you meet someone who is your soul mate,
the encounter is warmth.
It is incredible intimacy from the first minute,
an occasion in which everything flows
inexplicably easily and naturally,
and you are accepted for who you are.*

True love can only develop when it is coming from the heart, from the spiritual level. Medicine is constantly trying to convince us that the love organ is the brain and not the heart. Maybe physically it is so, I don't know that, but I know, with full certainty, that the spiritual center of love is the heart.

Scientists can measure biochemical and hormonal reactions in the brain. Nevertheless, it is again just one, although super powerful, computer. The heart is the spiritual center, the source of the inexplicable which constitutes love.

Working on our spirituality, we raise the vibration of our body to the level of the heart, fill in with light and become aware of who we are and what we want. It gives us the power to send universe a message of our higher consciousness, a signal which will resonate with someone who has the same heart vibration. That person is our soul mate. The message will attract him/her into our life. In contrast to lower, physical level of love, where we are attracted by people different from us, at the spiritual level we are attracted by and love similar people.

When you meet your soul mate, that encounter is warmth, incredible intimacy from the first minute, an occasion in which everything flows inexplicably easily and naturally, in which you are accepted for who you are.

If you meet someone and you want to present yourself different from who you are, better than you really are, it means that the person is not your soul mate.

No talking or explaining is necessary with your soul mate. The feeling that you complete each other is there even if you are in conflict, when there are disagreements, altercations and differences of opinion.

Problems and challenges will exist in love with a soul mate, too, because it isn't easy to be in a relationship with someone similar to us, but such disagreements motivate us to grow, improve, develop.

Most simply said, soul mates are members of one big spiritual family, a group of souls who splendidly complete each other and together fulfill the purpose of their existence. Those luckier among us meet more soul mates in their lifetime. These may be our children, parents, friends, partners... Those who haven't met any soul mates, permanently feel they are missing something, although they may not be aware what it is.

The majority have lost the ability to recognize their soul mate. This is partly because they are programmed by the fulfillment through physical love, and are *deaf and blind* for the vibrations and light coming from the heart. Also, partly because after many disappointments they stopped believing in love, like they stopped believing that there is God, Divine Energy, Higher Consciousness of the Universe, soul...

Joining two halves into one

The feeling of love comes entirely from joining two beings into one. Ancient Greek comedian Aristophanes in one of his pieces retells a myth where love is described as rejoining with our missing half. After that the life pain with which gods punished people for arrogance ceases. As the story says, at the beginning of the world we were double creatures: we had two heads, four legs, four arms... and then angry gods cut people in halves and scattered those halves all over Earth. Since then, people haven't felt true peace and happiness until they meet their other half and joined into one, unique and perfect being.

Thus spoke the Greeks. Egyptians have a similar story, and in the 19th century, British writer and politician Benjamin Disraeli named "our other half" the "antitype", and described love in this way: "He who finds his antitype enjoys a love perfect and enduring; time cannot change it, distance cannot remove it; the sympathy is complete." Chinese philosophy teaches us about joining seemingly disparate elements, yin and yang, male and female principles of nature into a complete One.

Souls – twins

Some soul mates are so similar as if they belong to the same person. Then we are talking about *twin souls*. These are identical souls which have constant spiritual contact, whether they are aware of that or not. If we have such a twin soul, we will always miss a part of ourselves, even if we are in a relationship with our soul mate with whom we have realised true love.

Separation from the twin soul often causes unfathomable moods and feelings, e.g. when we suffer or when we are happy and we don't know why. Our twin soul suffers somewhere else, and we can't help sharing that feeling no matter how far we are. How can we get in touch with another part of our soul? It is most often possible only when we aren't conscious, in a spiritual way, in our dream, because nine out of ten twin souls don't live on Earth at the same time, but exist in some other dimension.

True love never dies

The truth is that true love never dies and never stops existing. It is the energy which remains in the Universe eternally, it is our contact with the higher consciousness, God, the Creator.

Two people who really love each other, will do so forever. Their souls will remain connected and will meet in other lives because time is linear, but the soul is not. It lives forever in some other dimension.

When two souls love each other, when they really want to be together, their love will find the way to do so – in this, or in some other life. Just as there is no death of love, there is no unrealized love. If a love is real, it will always find the way to be realized. It is a love message in a bottle which will, even if it has to float over many oceans, always come to the right address!

Remember, love is eternal.
It never begins and it never ends.

Love at first sight

The prevailing fallacy is that genuine love is only the one at first sight, when "some special chemistry" is felt at the beginning, when you feel "jelly knees" looking at some man or woman.

It is that beating of your heart in your throat when s/he passes by.

It is that sweet lightheartedness when your eyes meet.

It is that fairy being which entered your life at one moment and which you cannot stop looking at.

It is that high moment, that encounter that electrifies and fascinates you.

That "chemistry" at first sight really exists but only rarely will there develop true love.

Even if it does, most often it hasn't been the first encounter of two souls, but a recognition, an encounter with the love which continues, revived love from some past lives.

It is something the soul knows and recognizes, from which all the excitement and bodily signals come, regardless of the fact that rationally we aren't aware of the spiritual dimension of the encounter.

At such a first encounter you intuitively feel that you know each other well, that you have already been together and that the person has been part of your life, although it is clear that you see him/her for the first time, and when your relationship begins, it feels as natural as if you have always been together.

My story

Conscious recognition that in this life we have met a soul we once loved in another life is quite rare. It happened to me when I met my husband. The moment our eyes met for the first time, I recognized him. That same evening I told my mother: "I met a man I'm going to marry."

Our love story proves that love has no boundaries and doesn't accept obstacles. My husband is from Croatia, I am from Israel. He was a professional athlete and was meant to get a long-term contract in one handball club in Finland. It failed because he broke his arm and canceled his journey. He was sad because of his discontinued career and the lost contract. After some time, quite unexpectedly, he received an offer to come and play in a club in Israel. And so he came to me. We met at a party and the spark between us flared up instantly.

My husband had never before even thought of possibly living in Israel, and when his sports career ended, we moved to Croatia together. Two wonderful children were born out of our love. Coral was born in Tel Aviv, and Darel was born in Zagreb.

My sister's story

My sister Lilach experienced a similar first encounter with her husband exactly here, in our house in Zagreb. It happened when she once came from Israel to visit us. Her previous marriage had ended and she was sad after the divorce. She wandered if she was ever to be happy again, to experience true love and she really worked much on herself, on raising to the vibration of the heart and removing her blockages. However, nothing happened.

That day we were walking in a park near my home, and when we stopped at the pond with gold fish, I encouraged her to wish for true love. When we came back home, the doorbell unexpectedly rang. She was nearer the door and went to open it, and there was my dear friend who accidentally called in because he was in the vicinity. When the two of them saw each other, it was like in the most romantic stories. It was just as if they were thunderstruck. They were standing still, staring at one another. And then, I introduced them to each other.

It is unbelievable how the two of them found each other. They are both well known in their respective countries and both have successful careers. My wonderful sister Lilach is an exquisite spiritual therapist and he is a famous musician. They didn't ask each other to sacrifice their way of life in the name of love. That is why, with their little girl, they live half a year in Israel, and half in Croatia.

The magical moon

You came with the full moon,
At the moment of magical light.
My heart beating with hope.
Love flared.
You awakened my soul.

I didn't know your name,
Didn't ask where you were coming from.
I only wanted to touch and feel
The union of souls.

Had we ever met before?
Had we ever touched before?
Did we know each other from another life?

I am looking into your eyes
Telling me you know.
Hold me strong,
And join me in the new vibration
Of the song
Born in our hearts.

It's dawn.
I can only wait
The next full moon,
When we meet
In the holly union. Again.

*Dawn has come and disappeared.
I remain impatient,
With a feeling of temptation.
I can only wait
For the new moon,
For our souls to touch.*

Iris Gattegno Tarbuk

Start by searching for happiness in yourself

When it isn't love at first sight or recognizing souls, but some ordinary first encounter which will start the course of introducing and developing a relationship, it generally looks like this:

First we estimate if s/he has everything we need. We present ourselves to each other in the best possible light. We see in each other what we want to see. We simply ignore what we might not like.

If we develop this new relationship further to a life together and marriage, that already described inevitable moment when we "open our eyes" arrives, except if it is a soul mate and true love in which we will accept our partner for who s/he is.

We are surprised and more and more disappointed. It isn't the same person we met, we grumble, criticize, reproach... We aren't aware that s/he has always been such, we just didn't want to see. The next step is to try and save the relationship by changing our partner. We want him/her to be like what we think s/he should be, but we are faced with a resistance. S/he is who s/he is, doesn't want to change, even tries to change and adjust us to his/her liking. We are getting angry, quarrel, conflicts grow.

From the female viewpoint, such a relationship is only an inevitable course of development of a girl who, as early as in puberty, starts creating a picture of her ideal man. As if she is making a shopping list. He has to be tall, handsome, clever, on top of it rich, of course, successful, well dressed and should drive a good car... When a woman decides to fall in love with someone, she expects that he will grant her wishes. If he fails to do that, she is terribly disappointed and bitterness and arguing begin.

When we are imagining the ideal man or the ideal woman, the list of their desirable characteristics usually contains what we ourselves are missing. We expect our partner to complete and make ourselves and our life in all its aspects perfect. Of course, we are disappointed when s/he fails. And, of course, it cannot succeed.

This is why the beginning of every successful relationship, as well as the necessary condition for experiencing true love is starting to change ourselves. When we love ourselves, when we have everything we need, we can only benefit from a love relationship, we can grow, develop, gain dignity and improve.

While searching for your soul mate, your true love, first search for happiness in yourself. That is of vital importance and that is why you should undertake everything you can to change your sad present-day situation, to stop the suffering of your life without love. To achieve that, do everything that may help you. Without prejudice. From faith, prayer, meditation, psychotherapy and talking to friends, to theta-healing treatments or therapeutic dance...

Chapter 3

LOVE AND SEX

*Sexual energy is the most powerful magic in the universe.
The woman and the man who know how to
raise that energy to the frequency of the heart,
unite love, magic and the truth.*

After the insight and experience of what true love is like and what it is, I asked *akasha* for an answer to the question why so few people experienced it.

Just as everything is only a symbol of some hidden secret, so the man and the woman have each their role in this world. The man is the symbol of the initial Provider – Creator, and the woman is the symbol of the initial Receiver – the Mother of Creation. Exactly the disruption of this circle of receiving and providing, and the fact that men and women, especially in Western civilization, have forgotten the meaning of the holy rite of union in which Divine Male and Divine Female principles join, have created a disruption of giving and receiving love through sex which deteriorated to the animalistic, physical level and remained limited only to so called first chakra. Meditating about that I received a surprisingly clear answer: the most responsible for this is – the woman!

Women who function from this lower, unconscious level, enter a sexual relationship with a need to feed on male energy and enter a love relationship in order to ensure a constant supply of male energy. Generally, neither men, nor women are aware of that.

Relationship between a man and a woman today is typically deviant. It isn't based on giving the energy of love, but is actually a battle of energies and exhaustion through sex.

Forgotten knowledge needs revisiting – both men and women need to learn how the woman can receive energy in sex and not exhaust the man, i.e. the man needs to learn how to exchange, and not to eject energy out of himself. In Eastern culture this ancient knowledge is preserved in *tao* love techniques, and in our part of the world teachings from the pre-Christian era have been eradicated. In Ancient Greece, the cult of Demetra was preserved, whose priestesses nurtured the knowledge of the holy sex and transferred that knowledge as the most precious one, to kings and dignitaries.

Inhibited true nature of the woman

In modern disrupted relationships, energy supply of the woman by the man looks like this: In the area of female lower chakras (pelvis, genitals, navel) there is a special energy formation. Since its form closely reminds me of an octopus, allow me to name it so. That *octopus* is placed in the sexual and reproductive part of woman's body, it has energy connection with the procreating sexual energy. It charges with energy in a sexual intercourse with the man. When it operates in accordance with its divine nature, the women, with its *octopus*, sucks in the energy the man voluntarily gives and elevates it through all her energy centers. So enriched, she returns it through her sexual center and gives it to the man so he can equally run it through all his energy centers and enrich himself with energy. That way, both partners in the relationship should feed with love. The woman instinctively remembers how to suck energy from the man because it is how the process starts, but both the woman and the man have more or less forgotten how to support the circulation of energy, how to light their inner light, how to close the circle of giving and receiving.

Thus in the majority of cases the sexual act between the man and the woman in a love embrace turns into something where the tentacles of this *octopus* from the woman's navel squirms towards the man's solar plexus chakra, the central energy chakra between his navel and his chest, and then tightly sticks to the man sucking his energy, feeding on him.

Nowadays it has become the prevailing form of energy exploitation between people. The woman lives from draining man's energy. However, since the "battery" hasn't lighted, the circuit hasn't been closed, it leaves the woman, and even more the man, unsatisfied. Typically, the man manages to get much less energy from the intercourse than he gave.

Sometimes, walking in the park, I come across embraced couples. They are seemingly happy, in love, and out of curiosity, I want to see if it is true love in some cases. However, when I open my third eye, almost as a rule, I see the insatiable *octopus* sucking his energy. Neither of them is happy. Energies are exchanged, they have gained something, but by far it isn't what they have expected. Therefore, both the man and the woman remain unsatisfied, insatiable, in constant search and anxiety...

Exhaustion of the man after sex

Such "feeding" takes place in every close, intimate touch between the man and the woman. Indeed, that need not be an outright sexual intercourse, but only a hug, a kiss... However, during the intercourse, this transfer of energy is strongest. Exactly there lies the answer to the question why men feel frail after a sexual intercourse. Why they are exhausted after sex, some of them being so drained that they are without any strength and immediately fall asleep. They transferred their whole energy to the woman, through the *octopus*.

And woman is, on the contrary, refreshed, energized, ready for more... she could talk and enjoy sex till dawn.

Such energy "robbing" doesn't exist when true love exists between the man and the woman. True love turns sexual intercourse into making love, where both lovers refresh with new energy, exchange energy with their whole bodies, "fill in" each other.

Sex is the most powerful magic in the universe

At the beginning of the world, the primordial woman had holy sexual energy, used it to rule over nature, brought wisdom and spirituality to the world and created new life. These were so called primitive societies, matriarchy, where women were priestesses and leaders. The woman was connected with Heaven, the man with Earth. Man's role was to activate the power of the primordial woman by making love to her. That is how they created offspring. It was known that making love was Holy Sex.

With the changes of civilisation, with the arrival of the era of male warrior domination, that primordial woman was suffocated. Due to her powers, that woman was persecuted, during the inquisition she was burned for being the witch, and her sexuality and reproductive organs were demonised and mutilated – in some parts of the world it is still the case. To survive, women hid and disacknowledged it, they were afraid to use it and in time, female energy being, once related to the spirituality of heavens, was downgraded to lower physical vibrations, and the relationship between the man and the woman distorted.

The woman was, indeed, forced to suppress her genuine nature, and to fulfill both her energy needs and life necessities, through the man. That is why today, instead of controlling it, the woman is controlled by her sexual energy.

In order to enjoy the completeness of her life, sex, true love, in order to bring spirituality to her family and the world, the modern woman needs to learn how to manage the energy of the *octopus*. In case she does not achieve that, only the love needed by the *octopus* will still dominate the consciousness of the woman – the lowest level of the satisfaction of her hunger through ordinary sex.

Sexual energy is the most powerful magic in the universe. The woman who knows how to raise that powerful energy to the frequency of the heart, knows how to put love and magic together. When they achieve such state, women are in the unending truth. This is why women today need to work on raising their female energy, especially those who have children, so that they are primarily women, and only after that, mothers, friends and everything else they want to be.

Woman as the robber of energy

In some women this *octopus* is stronger, in some it is weaker, some have totally mortified it... However, it isn't the result of some conscious effort they have made with a knowledge how to manage energy, but something that happens without involving their will nor consciousness.

Strong *octopus* gives the woman energy for which men desire them infatuated, run after them... She doesn't have to be pretty at all. The woman with a strong *octopus* can do whatever she wants with the man. Her strong energy attracts him because he believes that she will fulfill all his needs and that he will be happy with her.

When a women estimates that some man will be good energy food for her, she falls in love and says: *I love you, I cannot be without you.* And then, after her *octopus* has been fed, she never calls him again. This may seem rough and cheap, but exactly this gives rise to numerous dramas and love plots after which many men lose the will to live, are deeply disappointed in love, and it isn't rare that such relationships have a tragic end.

The man who likes a woman thinks like this: "Take from me whatever you want, but give me what I want, and it is – sex. "

The impulse is so strong in the man that to him it seems that sex isn't only a physical relief and a relief from tension and stress, but a direct contact with Divine Energy! That is why he falls for the *octopus*.

If from such relationships the man and the woman get married, they eventually typically don't even know why they did it. When you ask them, if concrete pressure from parents or the fact of pregnancy are lacking, the majority can't remember the reason at all.

As long as men and women consent to the control and program of the *octopus,* they can only have limited relationships and connections within that mode.

If they at the same time feel happy, they will feel they are in love.

If it lasts, they will think it is love.

If they get married, one day they will wake up miserable and unhappy.

When the man feels suffocated by such love and he wishes out, he will again look for another woman with a strong *octopus* energy and will again think that he has gained something, that he touched the skies. And in reality, he will only again enter the same circle of physical relationship and energy exploitation between the sexes without true love, and waste energy because he doesn't know how to respond to woman's demands, especially not to the demands of a woman with a strong *octopus*.

Every woman with a strong octopus has a strong potential for spiritual growth. It depends on her alone if she raises it to higher centers, to the heart, or she uses it to catch men and take their energy. Such a woman is not culpable for having the powerful energy in the first chakra, but it would be good if she knew how to use it. In case she does not possess the knowledge, that energy titillating her will lead her through life, the same as when a man is led through life by his sexual appetites.

Men unconsciously know about the existence of the *octopus*, sense the danger that the woman will feed on them. It can be clearly seen in situations when a women enters the space occupied by men, e. g. in some pub. Till that moment everybody is engaged in a relaxed conversation, but at the moment she enters, they spontaneously direct their hands towards their solar plexus, as if they want to defend against her *octopus*. Solar plexus is the center for energy exchange between people, and that is exactly why the *octopus* aspires exactly to that chakra of the man.

Such defensive reaction will happen instinctively towards every woman in whom men sense a strong octopus, no matter how pretty and attractive she is. Only after she sits down in the company of somebody else, when there is no danger any more, this anxiety they are feeling will vanish, and they will relax again.

Energy of the successful man

I have lately been noticing more and more men with an *octopus*, although it is really rare. Such a strong energy is especially possessed by some successful men and that is why women they win over look like they have been paralyzed by something and headless.

On the other hand, I know some women who totally put their *octopus* out. They only transmit their heart frequency. They won't find love either, because their signals are typically not recognized by men, and such women actually don't attract them.

Samson and Delilah

Past is rich with stories about women with a strong *octopus* who tailored the world history. I will mention only some legends and events which are continuously an inspiration for writers and artists to write best-sellers, paint masterpieces, shoot movie spectacles... because such women fascinate all people in all periods of our history.

One of them is the Biblical story about Samson and Delilah. Samson was a Jewish boy who dismembered a lion with his bare hands. The saying is that the source of his strength was his long hair. The celebrated hero fell in love with the Philistine Delilah, member of the most fierce enemy of his people, paid to disclose the secret of his strength. Fascinated by Delilah, obsessed with the need to have her surrendered (I would say – subdued by her *octopus*), satisfied her wish to tell her the secret of his strength as a token of his love. He disclosed his biggest secret, and when he fell asleep exhausted after sex, Delilah cut his hair. She delivered weak Samson, without the source of his super-human strength to the soldiers. For joining with her *octopus* he paid with his own life.

Cleopatra – ugly and fatal

While the story about Samson and Delilah is only a Biblical myth on the eternal theme of the frightening female sexual power over a physically strong man, Cleopatra was a real historical person. Since two biggest Roman army leaders were in love with her, Cleopatra's exquisite beauty is assumed and celebrated, but historical evidence tells us that the famous Egyptian beauty queen wasn't beautiful at all. Preserved sculptures and relief shape reproduced in coins and medallions from her era, prove that she was a woman with a disproportionately big nose, straight lips and sharp jaw. Her contemporaries didn'tt consider her to be even close to some romantic heroine as we present her today, and old Roman authors of chronicles described her as "a dangerous woman who by sex, deceit and witchcraft ruled over men". Certainly, one of the most charismatic women in the world history. The fact that she succeeded in captivating two most powerful men of her time is still fascinating. These two men, for the love of her, ensured that the throne of Egypt went to her.

She was 24 when she tried to take over the rulership from her younger brother-husband Ptolemy XIII. After that, exiled from Alexandria, Cleopatra formed an army of Syrian mercenaries and came to pharaoh's capital lurking for an opportunity to attack. Roman general Julius Caesar, in charge of the stability of Egypt, ruled in Alexandria at the time. He invited the brother and the sister to reconcile, but the pharaoh refused. Counting on Caesar to help her ascend the throne, Cleopatra ordered her servant to roll her up in a carpet and carry it as a present to Caesar. When Caesar received it, the servant unrolled the carpet in front of him, and in that charming but dramatic choreography, the Egyptian queen prostrating herself before him. By this unique and brave act, Cleopatra captivated the roman soldier. With his support she became the ruler of Egypt, and she gave birth to the future Roman Emperor's son. When her protector was assassinated in front of the Roman Senate, she captivated another Roman General, Mark Anthony by embarking on his warship dressed as Roman goddess of love, Venus. She gave birth to three of his children, they lived and ruled Egypt together, defying the Roman Empire. Emperor Octavian defeated Mark Anthony's army, and from Roman soldiers, Cleopatra hid in the tomb she had built for herself. Mark Anthony learned that she died and he took his life by falling upon his sword. Cleopatra, hearing of his death, committed suicide by putting her hand in the basket with a poisonous cobra inside. The asp bit her and this brought Cleopatra death.

Insatiable Catharine the Great

Russian Empress, Catharine the Great became famous in history for her insatiable sexual appetite. As a young Prussian princess, she was brought to Russia to marry Duke Peter, future Russian Tsar, a youth whose mental and physical powers were at the level of a boy. Since he wasn't capable of ensuring heir to the throne, his mother, Russian Empress Elizabeth, in line with the then habitute, allowed Catherine to have lovers and thus give birth to a child.

When she become the empress, Catherine started using her unlimited sovereign powers to obtain sexual services from young soldiers, and she got rid of Peter – he abdicated, and soon after that, he died under obscure circumstances. Although her rule was of fateful importance for Russia, where she expanded its borders to the Black Sea and Central Europe and modernized the country (her era is also called golden age), she became world famous for her insatiable sexual appetite.

Why men accept to be energy food for women

Most love relationships rest on energy exploitation, on the *octopus*. In such relationships neither women nor men are really happy, but they find it difficult to become aware of the process and change it, because since their early age, they have got used to the program of the *octopus* by their mothers. This is why there are few of those who manage to cross over to the program of the heart or feel in any way such a fine and high vibration in a woman, feel attracted to such a woman and experience true love.

Almost every man learns from his mother to obey the woman, bend to her will, fulfill her wishes and orders, be good so she loves him. It is integral to men, like an instinct. They are also programmed to search for a woman who will stick her *octopus* onto them, they don't know of a love different from such energy connection.

Still, men have a significant advantage over women – contrary to them, they don't mix up sex with love. Many among them don't even crave love, because sex which they receive with energy exchange with the *octopus* will suffice. Thereby, they are aware that they participate in a game in which somebody always "chases and catches" them.

Men are players and sportsmen, and so they like to play with the *octopus*, although they know that one day they will be caught. For that reason they want to be free as long as possible, and they say: "All right.

I know that you want to feed on me, but then, I want to play and enjoy it." However, when they get married, playing ceases. That is the reason why men are afraid of marriage, while women always want it, since by marriage they get a permanent source of man's energy, her food.

Mothers should teach their girls and boys to love and accept themselves from an early age. It is really difficult to achieve that in girls since we are still struggling with our collective consciousness which constrains the primordial energy of the woman. From their early age, for girls sexual and love energy is the one they get through the *octopus*. For them, sex is food and energy and love. It is exactly their mothers who have to help them and teach them to discern between the energy of sex and the energy of love.

Although many women aren't happy existing like this, they mostly go on with their lives in the most comfortable way, i.e. without putting any efforts into change. They live their lives surrendered to their *octopus* control to the very end, without asking anything more from the man than a relationship "*I give you – you give me*".

You can recognise them by their constant dissatisfaction with love. Bitterly talking that love is suffering, drama and adversity, they say: *"Love hurts"*, instead of *"All we need is love"*.

If love brings you pain, look into yourself.

Where do you feel love? In your heart, stomach, or...

Transform love pain into unconditional love coming from the heart.

Don Juan – toxic dependence

Playing with the *octopus*, many men get so involved in the play, that they turn into real game addicts, they become seducers, erotomaniacs, womanizers. They enter into relationships with many women, but such relationships don't bring them real, deep permeating satisfaction and peace they crave for, but only a momentary pleasure.

Men who slept with many women are emotionally empty inside and dissatisfied. They are always missing, they are constantly frustrated, bitter, disappointed. When I look at their aura, i. e. energy field around their body, I see it is full of holes, cavities and cracks which become more numerous and larger with more years of living so.

Womanizers are men who are obsessively hungry for the *octopus*. One impersonation of such a man is the historical and literary hero, seducer of women, Don Juan. His love life was described like an undertaking for which other men envied him, while in reality, he was miserable and unhappy, sick. We call such a form of relationships of men with women Don Juan syndrome. A man like he was cannot be without women, and at the same time, he wants to take a revenge on them. Seducer, erotomaniac, womanizer, Don Juan is deeply aware of the fact that women suck his energy through his solar plexus and it is his moral justification to do what he does: "I know that you are going to feed on me, and I will punish you for that. I will use you and discard you. I will punish you and all the women who exploited me my whole life and who intend to exploit me."

What actually happens with energies in such a relationship? The man – avenger takes the woman. In their love embrace she puts her *octopus* onto him and starts taking his energy. During that activity, the *octopus* is not equally strong all the time. The man uses occasional weakness of the woman's *octopus* so that through his solar plexus he pours his "poison" into her. That "poison", sent to the woman through her *octopus* by the man – avenger, works like some sort of a drug which will generate her complete dependence on him. Exactly that Don Juan's "poisonous substance" will cause the woman to fall in love with him head over heels, ready to forgive him everything, deeply humiliate herself just to keep him, madly suffer and even decide to commit a suicide.

By-standers are surprised by his cruelty and her folly, they curl their lip in contempt at such a relationship. Neither Don Juan nor the seduced women are aware of the real mechanisms at work here. Neither of them is happy in the relationship. The relationship becomes hellish suffering for both.

Is there, nonetheless, some exit from that hell? There is. Both need to change the program on which they utilize their energy. When they raise it to the heart frequency, they will be saved.

Love without sex, sex without love

You will sometimes hear men who were in love and adored their wives, lived in happy marriages, swore eternal love, saying all of a sudden: "I don't love her any more! I'm disgusted by sex with her. She neglected herself, she doesn't attract me any more!"

How can that be? That is the same person, the same body you were in love with. If there is true love between the two of you, then the old, fat, thin and sick body of the one you love, attracts you all the same.

Indeed, this wasn't love, but only sex which he named love.

Love and sex are driven by totally different energies. Sex with the person we love is spiritual, holy, it is love making. It brings spiritual and physical consolidation. That is why various heterosexual and homosexual variations of love relationships with or without sex are possible. For example, one man may need sex with another man, and at the same time be in a sexless love relationship with a woman.

Ordinary sex is only a form of energy exchange through the *octopus*, it isn't related to love. Such sex is a mere share of energy needs. Most people make the mistake of confusing it with love. It seems rude to say, but the truth is that ordinary sex is only a simple physical act, satisfaction of a physical need, something animals do as well. Something that is relaxing, relieving, fun. There is nothing wrong in having such sex, but don't consider it to be love. Be aware what need it is and how you will satisfy it.

It is unlucky when one partner, and it is usually the woman, confuses ordinary sex with love. Then there are broken hearts, bad feelings, depression. Only sometimes, very rarely, sex may be a foundation on which true love will eventually develop, when both have raised their frequency to the heart level and thus entered the energy of love.

The price of coupling with a woman

There are many men who are scared of women (by this I don't mean those pathological cases belonging to the psychiatric domain). Fundamental fear men feel towards women emerges from their intuitive knowledge that coupling with a woman won't be for free. They know that they will pay some price, they just don't know what currency and what amount it will be. When both the woman and the man relate "heart to heart", then there are no fears, no distress, no hell of addiction. Exchange of energies is easy and good, both at the level of the *octopus* and at the level of the heart. Even in such a relationship, in true love, there is pain, but it is pure pain which is a part of a normal, healthy relationship of two people who love each other. Then we can claim that the woman and the man have by their relationship restrained the *octopus*, "tamed" it and put it in the service of true love.

Energy recovery with alcohol

Looking into history, you will see that only few got married for love, although love has always been sought. Ancient Greeks waged the ten-year Trojan war allegedly for love. But there was no love between Helen and Paris – it was playing with energies. Ancient Greek beauty had a strong *octopus*, just like Cleopatra and Catherine the Great. Such women deprive the man from so much energy that they exhaust him. He usually recovers his energy either with other women or with alcohol.

There is one such couple I know, seemingly so incompatible that nobody who gets to know them can understand how these two people got together in the first place, let alone that they have been married for more than twenty years. He is an outstanding intellectual of the world rank, while she is a very primitive, uneducated woman with bad manners. Regardless of the situation and the company they are with, they kiss and touch each other, exchange sexual allusions so that everybody feels embarrassed. He isn't happy, drinks on a daily basis and in front of all people who love him, he is wasting away, but is unable to leave his wife. And she shines, radiates with energy, proudly strutting with her husband as if he were her prey. It is a woman with strong sexual energy, with a powerful *octopus*. That is why he is like hypnotized and totally weak with her, and his great intelligence and competences in all other areas cannot help him there. Since she is greatly exhausting him, he is trying to compensate at least a part of his energy with alcohol. The only thing that might help him is if his wife started working on herself cleansing her energy and thus raising to the vibration of the heart. When her center of energy is her heart, i.e. when his wife isn't dominated by the *octopus*, he will be in balance, too. Only then their relationship will either grow into true love or both will have enough strength to break.

However, I cannot give an answer to the question how to reach the point where she would want such a change.

He might be rescued if he gets sick and thus stops being interesting food for her, and she catches another man.

Chapter 4

SPIRITUALITY OF THE WOMAN AND THE MAN

The essence of the division of sexes in this world is that women need to bring spirituality of Heaven, while men bring the spirituality of Earth. In this relationship nobody should be victimized.

Equality between women and men is wonderful and nobody should be victimized in this relationship. I believe that the division of sexes in this world is such that women need to bring to this world the spirituality of Heaven, while men bring the spirituality of Earth.

It doesn't mean that women are closer to God since we are all equally close to God, but spirituality comes to the planet through the woman. This is why men work more and take care of providing for the family, while women take care about the spirituality in the family.

Balance of sex and heart energies

The life such as led by the majority of today's women and men is giving up on spirituality. Women are extinguished goddesses and restrained priestesses living in an imbalance of the body and the soul.

Most women delegate the choice of the man to the *octopus* which is driven only by its energy appetite: *"You are fine food for me, I'll take you."*

If the man isn't strong, the women wins and feeds on him. If she concludes that he has been good food, she will marry him.

Years are passing by, and then the alarm, warning that something is not good, goes off. But they are already so busy with their everyday life, feeding the *octopus* and sustaining lower frequencies, that they are turning a deaf ear to the alarm and change nothing.

Nonetheless, inwardly, they pulsate with a sinister feeling that something is wrong. Since they don't know what is wrong, they start being dissatisfied. Women sometimes fall sick with gynaecological diseases, or suffer from infertility or enter the premature menopause. Men start being tortured by problems of impotence or prostate diseases.

It happens to both women and men because they use their sexual energy in a wrong way which prevents their spiritual development. I need to repeat the very important fact: the woman and the man are happy only when they establish the balance of sexual and heart energies. Then they are creative, spiritual, attract love, give and receive energy – and remain healthy.

Beauty isn't important in the love between souls

Today's society of mass media and a rigid collective consciousness are putting pressure on us, so we have to judge what the man and the woman look like, to acquire attitudes about what they should look like and then, according to that, decide if that man or if that woman is a good choice for us. That is creating a viewpoint which leads to untruth and unhappiness. True love isn't bothered by overweight. Our soul mate can be a disabled person. True love cannot be obstructed because the girl doesn't have breasts for a bra size 34. In a true relationship between soul mates, the beauty and the looks are really not important. And when it isn't the case? This story is about it:

One beautiful girl, a successful model, fell in love with a very handsome and successful man. They were a perfect couple. That is what everybody who knew them thought, and that is how they saw themselves. They got married and the love bloomed till the moment she had a car accident. She was seriously injured. A broken arm and a broken leg, injured spine, brain concussion. After a long and difficult rehabilitation, she came home in a wheelchair.

Their married life was short-lived. One day her husband packed his stuff and said: "I cannot be with you any more. I don't love you any more." He left her.

Real truth surfaced. That man had never loved that woman. They were together in the *octopus* program, in the program of the *hunter* and the *hunted*, in the program *"I will take you"*. He left her because now her body wasn't what he wanted to have. You don't leave the person you truly love because s/he is physically different.

This is, indeed, an extreme example, but it is real, and it is life. Many people get married while in love only with the other person's beautiful body or because s/he is successful at work or has much money and a good car. When that disappears, their "love" disappears.

A case contrary to the described above. I know a happy married couple where the man fell in love with a girl who was in the wheelchair due to cerebral paralysis. The illness wasn't the biggest obstacle to their love, but his mother who couldn't accept that her healthy, handsome and promising son could marry a handicapped, sick woman, about whom he will have to take care their whole life. These two, nevertheless, married, although it was against the mother's will.

Love after serious illness

Sometimes we witness how somebody experiences luck, true love, after s/he has survived a serious disease. What happens when a person falls sick? S/he starts asking questions about his/her life, starts searching for answers, starts opening up for spirituality, for higher consciousness. Indeed, a serious disease is a path to opening up for many people and after a recovery, they raise to the frequency of the heart and find true love.

After such a change, it happens to both women and men that with different eyes they see someone whom, in some earlier encounter they dismissed as a possible partner, because his or her appearance or economic or social status didn't match their wish and ideal. They start respecting that person and the new encounter develops into a genuine love relationship and a happy marriage.

There is one such story which happened right before writing this book. She is a modest cashier, and he is a plumber. They are young people of the same age. They were in a short relationship which was terminated due to her overweight. It was something he finally didn't like. They parted quietly, and they seemed to have forgotten each other. In the meantime, he fell sick with a serious and incurable disease. He got into a wheelchair. For several years he hopelessly suffered awaiting the final exacerbation of the disease and sure death, and then he was invited to participate in the experimental group for a new medicine testing. Out of the fifteen included patients, the new drug helped only him and one other patient. And so, he was on his feet again. He started walking again and returned to life. He started going out, going fishing with his friend, and he again joined Facebook. There he came across his ex love and contacted her. They agreed to meet.

Seeing the soul

She wasn't much changed. Surplus kilos were still there, but now he saw a completely different person. He changed spiritually. With the awakened spirituality after the serious disease, he didn't see her physical body, but her soul. Moreover, he now discovered some magnificent characteristics she had. True love was born, they started living together, and they married after a few months. His disease remained incurable, existing in him, but sleeping now and letting him live normally, and she was still chubby with all the flaws which he couldn't stand before. But they are enjoying their love, they are more than happy and are waiting for their baby. At one time, that young man had nothing, but that painful experience enabled him to have everything now. I was most touched when the bride, happy and out of breath after a whole night of dancing in her long white wedding dress, excitedly said: "Finally, something nice happened to me!"

Angels are seen through heart

It is a pity that all who face such a serious disease or some other difficult life challenge don't succeed in achieving such spiritual improvement. Some become bitter, hating other people and the whole world. And those whose hearts are enlightened, become really special persons: they develop the ability of intuition, they often open their *third eye*, start seeing with *different eyes*, actually with a different organ – their heart. Their reality and picture of the world become completely different from what they were before the illness.

My son Darel can see energies, he is very intuitively gifted, to such an extent that, unlike me, he can see angels. When he sees a girl who can be the ugliest creature in the world for someone else, my son says: "Mum, look how pretty this girl is. When I walk with her, everybody will look at us." He really sees her beauty because he only looks at her soul. That is how couples who have true love look at each other. When you really love, you don't see the age, the baldness, neither small breasts, thin lips, fat legs are important. You are overflown with the light from that person's heart and you can only see her/his soul. One girl literally didn't see that her beloved was bald, although he was even when they had met. When they had already been married for some time, at one dinner party their friends started talking about his hair. She was surprised, as if then she saw him for the first time.

People who are pure love

People among us who only care about what someone's soul is like, are rare. And when we die, only that which was our soul goes with us to the other world. Physicality, which is only a shell for our souls, disappears. Both the most beautiful model and the ugliest girl become only *dust* after death.

God won't ask you how much you earned, not even how many times you went to church in your lifetime. In your soul, God will see how you lived and loved, what you did in your life, how many people you made happy, how many people you helped. Is it not exactly that what gives our living the beauty and the meaning?

Our body sets obstacles to achieving the ideal of unconditional love. There are people who are pure love, who overcome physical constraints.

For example, when at the railway station in Calcutta Mother Theresa kissed the poor man's feet, dusty, dirty and disfigured by illness, she expressed pure love for God. In every human being she could see the soul only, without his or her physical shape. It is something possible to only few people, so few that I have never met anyone who could so overcome the corporeal.

The fact is that many people talk about God and love and often go to church, as they are constantly wrapped in hatred, gossip and malice towards others. I cannot teach you what is God, nobody can do that because God is personal experience, which is why some name it God, some Divine Energy, some Higher Consciousness, Universal Consciousness... No matter how we name it, I know that the path to God's love isn't only a mere wish, need, or a must, but is the path leading to touching the eternity where our soul exists.

Therefore, the most important thing we have to do in order to connect with God, Divine Energy and Universal Consciousness is to become aware of our spirituality, work on our heart – raise its frequency, fill it with light.

I sometimes see marriages where the relationship between the man and the woman doesn't flow through the *octopus*, but through the heart, the place where men and women develop their spirituality together, sometimes unaware of that. Spirituality is not associated with your work on that or with going somewhere, nor with doing some prescribed rituals, but is associated with how you live your everyday life, what you think, how you share your life together, what and how you eat, do...

Spouses who are connected at the heart level, build spirituality in their home, and then their children are different, too. They are children who think about others, respect them, don't swear, they aren't aggressive, don't have a tendency to start smoking, drinking, using drugs. A very special energy can be felt in the home of such a family, which isn't impossible to achieve, you can all do it.

Spiritual sex

Making love is holy, spiritual sex. It is something people of old times were aware of, and it is totally forgotten today. While we are making love, it is sex during which we feel all the levels of our soul and our body being in contact with our lover.

Those who are able to see auras during love making, see an explosion of colors melting around the lovers. Couples who really love each other have holy sex and can break through the secret of love making. Some achieve that feeling of touching souls so that they look each other in the eyes during love making. Others enjoy that they are guided only by their senses in total darkness. I advise that before love making with your partner you focus on your heart as the centre of your body. Ask yourself why you want to join your energy to your partner's and then allow your energies to mix, without physical touch. Repeat this several times during the next few days and only when you feel you are ready, abandon yourself to the holy sex. During love making think about how you are raising your energy to the heart level.

"Even in death, we shall forever hold hands"

Love between the ingenious Spanish painter Salvador Dali and the Russian Gala started at first sight. He was twenty-five, and she was eleven years older. In his memoirs, the painter describes that first encounter with the love of his life, like this: "The moment I saw her, I felt she was my friend."

They lived together for fifty-two years and during all this time they weren't separated for a day. They were only separated by her death. Gala was Dali's muse and eternal inspiration: "She is very clever, she completely understands me. Her skin isn't firm and she is older than I, sometimes she is very ugly. But I still love her. Now, here tomorrow, there, and when we die, when we are no more, we shall still hold hands. Forever."

Dali could not get over Gala dying first and leaving him alone. Four years after her death, losing his will to live, getting weak, he died, too. He didn't eat nor drink putting himself into a state of hallucinating in which he could talk with Gala when their souls would meet in some space between the worlds: "I deliberately parched myself so as to get into the state of consciousness in which I could see her. She would stand in front of me, as defiant as only she could be."

Chapter 5

CONTACT WITH THE SOUL OF YOUR LOVED ONE WHO DIED

People who died want us to continue with our lives

because they know that death is an illusion

and that time doesn't exist.

We are all here for eternity.

Although contacts with the soul of a deceased are a taboo topic in the contemporary culture, especially Western culture, an increasing number of people talk openly about such experience and contacts. Thanks to the development of technology, many prove them by night audio and video recordings from the rooms where they sleep, and where they were visited by the souls of the deceased. That relation between "this" and the "afterworld" really exists.

That is because true love never dies. After the death of the loved one it is possible to connect with his/her soul. How? Through a prayer, meditation, with the help of a spiritual medium or in dreams.

After death, the soul leaves the body and with all its feelings it continues to exist in another dimension. Someone you deeply love and with whom you are profoundly connected has been separated from you by death forever. Now you are hurting because you miss him/her very much, you would do anything to continue the relationship, you acutely wish to talk to that person again, but it seems impossible and only pain remains. However, it isn't exactly so, death isn't the end of everything. Indeed, it is possible to connect with the deceased loved one.

First, you have to know and be aware that the soul of the loved one wants to get in touch with you. In order that the connection is realised, you need to unconditionally believe that it is possible. If you want to get in touch with the soul of a deceased person, you will achieve that only if you believe with all your heart that it is possible and you need to eagerly pray for that contact. Pray the way you usually do, in agreement with your beliefs, your prayers patiently building the bridge between the worlds and enabling such contacts.

If it was true love, and if the soul of the deceased, in its dimension, prays for a contact with you, it will happen. Be patient – however the experience may be new and painful for you, it is as new and painful for the soul of the deceased. Accept the fact that the concept of time flow doesn't exist in their dimension, that only we who are in this world have time as a determiner of existence and that our worlds exist parallel, separated by dimensions only.

If you are aware of that and if you are really unconditionally open to the possibility of contacting the loved one who is in the otherworld, you will be able to recognise the sign!

Signs of the presence of the soul of the deceased

There are many different signs which the souls of the deceased send when they want to get in touch with us. For example, such a sign can be when on the radio you hear the music which you both liked to listen to. Or when the film you watched together is on TV... Souls of the deceased often use electricity to communicate with our dimension. So, an even clearer sign can be the light which turns on and off by itself, or a TV set turning on or off while we are talking about that person. Some people get a strange call on their mobile phone – the caller's number is the same as the number used by the deceased person when s/he was alive.

To be able to recognise the signs, you need to be fully open for all the possibilities. It reminds me of the anecdote about Indians who saw Columbus' ships approaching the American soil for the first time. They saw them, but they didn't perceive them! Never before had they seen a ship or such people coming from the sea. What they saw didn't exist for them because they weren't open for any possibility of such people coming to their shores. That is why they could not perceive the ships. Only when the first of them said that he saw people coming from the sea, others perceived the ships, too.

There is one wonderful example of my clients. These people were in terrible pain – their daughter Emma lost her life in a traffic accident. Only a couple of weeks before her death, together they had bought a pet – a parrot. After the accident, the bird suddenly started saying: "Emma is here! Emma is here!" They were surprised, but they recognised that Emma took that path to stay in touch.

Accomplishing a contact

Imagine that death cut off the telephone connection you daily used to talk with your love. However, telephone isn't the only possibility to communicate. You can get through and stay in touch via other means of communication, like a telegram, letter, e-mail. You will establish some new way of communication, but it takes time to find the address, to send a letter, for the letter to reach the receiver. Although via the phone you talk but you don't hear each other – you don't hear that person, and that person doesn't hear you, you need to believe the other still exists, talks, only you cannot hear him/her right now. What I want to say is that if you don't see or hear someone, it doesn't mean s/he doesn't exist or isn't well.

You need to be patient, to wait for the connection to be established and be ready for the contact. It is important that you don't get scared if it happens. By no means should you start shouting: "You are dead! You don't exist!" The deceased may see it as a message that you are scared of him/her, and may decide not to scare or disturb you any more. You may lose all chances to contact the loved one again. This is why you shouldn't panic if you hear the voice of the deceased. Contact with a soul or a spirit should be like your usual contacts: you can talk, hold hands, hug or even make love in that space between the worlds.

Dreams and the zone between the dream and reality are an area where two worlds merge, two dimensions where such encounters most often happen and where it is easiest for both persons to connect. Sometimes it is in deep sleep, sometimes in half-awake, somnolent state at the beginning or at the end of sleep, the way described in the chapter about contact with your soul mate in dreams. That is why audio and video camera recordings may prove that presence and contact.

Such contacts are very tiring for the souls of the deceased. It is a long way to move over from their dimension to our level of existence, and they spend much of their energy. So, don't expect constant encounters with them, but try to communicate with them telepathically, by sending and receiving mental messages. As a spiritual medium, I realise such a contact with the souls. Asleep, when I leave my physical body, I meet them at the astral plane. Then I see them as they looked while they lived. They are young and beautiful.

In that world, everybody is young again.

Saying goodbye with the help of a spiritual medium

It is possible to get in touch with the loved one who deceased with the help of a spiritual medium. My ability to communicate with the souls of the deceased emerged after a young man I loved in my youth had died. After that I started receiving telepathic messages from other people who had messages for their loved ones who had been crying and mourning after them in this world. They wanted to console them, to tell them they were well where they were, communicate something important they hadn't managed to do in their lifetime...

Sometimes I receive a message totally unexpectedly, while I am alone preparing dinner at home, and when I run workshops for a group of people, I feel the presence of their close loved ones who died, asking me to convey a message. These are such warm, human stories, sometimes small things, like they wanted to warn that the plumbing in the house was bad and might break; or to say that it was important for them that the watch they had gotten from their father be kept.

At one workshop I got a message for a woman dressed in black and felt a wonderful smell of apple pie with cinamon. Her deceased husband wanted me to convey his widow the message that he was by her watching her. In such a situation, as a spiritual medium, I have to decide if the person is ready for such communication. She was so sad, and he so much insisted that I should convey the message, that I told her he wanted to communicate with her through me. However surprised and scared she was, she wanted that, too. He told her that he was watching her as she was crying at home and that he knew she was sleeping on his side of the bed after his death. He asked her to stop mourning, because their children suffered – they couldn't live normally. He thanked her for the wonderful life they had had together and said that he was missing her apple pie with cinamon, that he would always love her, that they would be together again, but that in this life she had to accept his death and continue with her life.

She was weeping terribly while I was telling her his messages. If she doubted that it was really him talking to her, that doubt disappeared when he said he knew she had been sleeping on his pillow. She was astounded, but she accepted the message and promised she would stop mourning for him. I continued talking with others at the workshop when suddenly I received another greeting for her. I cautiously asked her: "Madam, did you have a dog?" They really had a dog who died two weeks after her husband. The message for the widow was that they were well and that they were together.

Still, the most touching experience I have had was with a young woman who visited me desperate, three days after the sudden death of her husband. She received the message through me that she shouldn't weep since part of him stayed with her, their child being conceived two weeks ago. That was something she least expected. When after two weeks she called me to confirm the good news, her happiness was infinite.

I believe that it would be nice and necessary to have a farewell ceremony for the deceased not only with the priest at the funeral service, but also through the mediation of a spiritual medium. Although the priest is a spiritual medium of a kind, s/he is more oriented to the ritual. It would be nice and necessary that the soul of the deceased person and the family and friends say goodbye with the help and mediation of a spiritual medium. Those who remain here will become aware that they are parted only from the body of the deceased and that the soul of the loved one is still alive and their ties and communication are not severed now. That way death would be easier for both the deceased one and for those who remain after him/her. I hope I will live long enough to see that.

Although there are people who are spiritual mediums and through them you can contact your loved ones who died, it is of utmost importance that you yourself develop the ability to receive signs, recognize messages, encounters... to work on yourselves, instead of becoming dependent on visiting spiritual mediums.

The deceased affecting our lives

People don't turn into angels for the mere fact of being physically dead, they don't improve merely because their souls now live in another, higher dimension. They change in time. If the deceased was a bad person, s/he will remain one.

For example, if the deceased loved you, s/he often tries to affect your life by finding you a partner with whom you might live on happily, instead of mourning after him/her. When I mediate in such contacts, the soul of the deceased often sends a message for the loved one to stop mourning and being alone. Of course, there are jealous spirits who don't want their wife or husband to have a new partner. It may go pretty far, like when the spirit of the deceased physically attacks the new partner, hitting him/her even painfully, the moment s/he approaches the widow/er.

Sometimes you love, but the deceased doesn't share the love and doesn't want to get in touch. If you persist in invoking him/her with your prayers, s/he may get angry, become unpleasant, cause some bad things in your life. That is why you should be cautious as to with whose spirit from the world of the dead you are invoking a contact.

Souls of our loved ones know what is good for us, and what isn't. They come when we need help, if we ask for that. They also help by praying for us in their dimension, and at the moment of our death, they come for us to ease our soul's transition to the other dimension.

However, spirits are limited in their actions. They can sometimes help us in our life troubles and dilemmas, but they cannot be at our disposal all the time, however much they may wish that. We need to live our earthly lives ourselves. They, in the other dimension, also have their lives to live.

Dream time

He:

*The first rain is mixing with my tears.
Drops are drumming.
Blended with the cold soil,
I see you in the mist.*

She:

*I am surrounded by your scent,
And you left to another world.
Your pain has finished,
Mine is only starting.
Shedding tears,
I can still hear you.*

Together:

*Waiting for the sunset,
Waiting for the night
Waiting for dreams
To reunite*

She:

*My love,
I'm here to embrace your heart.
Let me be with you,
Let me hold you.*

I am here, by you.
We shall never part.
For eternal love like ours,
Separation is only temporary.

He:

In dreams we are united forever.
Another world, other rules.
But my love for you
Always looms alive
More than ever.

Together:

My love,
We are together forever.
Our love
Dispels the mist.
I shall love you forever.
In dreams
We shall be joined forever.

Iris Gattegno Tarbuk

Chapter 6

ATTRACTING THE SOUL MATE

*If we blame only other people
for our personal failures,
we will get stuck on the wrong life path,
unable to progress.*

Until now we have been focused on making the difference between true love and the illusion of love, ordinary and spiritual sex, i.e. sexual intercourse and love making. We have described relationships between the sexes and love partners, dangers and consequences of a wrong choice of a partner. Now I am going to give you concrete advice about how to attract your soul mate and realize real, true love.

Before you start working on attracting love into your life, it is important to know what you want from love, what you want from a partner. I'm not talking about childhood or adolescent love, about a fascination with some actor/actress from a blockbuster movie or a TV series, nor about the enchantment with the prettiest or most handsome classmate or neighbour in puberty.

I'm not talking about adventure, disengaged relationship, sex because you are weak at some time, neither sex because you need it or for fun. I am talking about seeking to find and make a serious choice of a love and life partner.

Is he the one? Is she the woman of my life?

You are already in love, feelings are strong, you are in the seventh heaven, floating in the clouds, you feel butterflies fluttering in your stomach, shivers down your spine... But there is doubt smoldering in your heart – is it true love or a transient enchantment, does s/he love as much as I do, is it something to last, or is it just an affair?

How will you know if s/he is the one? First, think about how much you really know the person. Clear your head as much as possible and make a list of your partner's characteristics that you like. If the list is short it shows that you don't know much about the person, or s/he doesn't have the characteristics which would be worthy of your attention, then it is clearly love at the physical level, namely, a temporary enchantment with a possible bad ending.

If the list is longer, you should seriously talk with that person about life interests and goals.

If he likes folk music. while you like the opera; if you like to walk in the woods and idyllic villages, while he likes cafés and city turbulence; if you have recognizably disparate interests – he enjoys eating meet while you are a strict vegetarian – then everything will be clear.

Of course, it may be true love, the one which transforms the foundations of a personality, the one for which we are willing to embrace a new way of life and existence. However, one shouldn't forget that in such situations, at the beginning we present ourselves in the best of light and we both conceal who we really are.

What if s/he doesn't notice you

If you are suffering because you love someone who does not respond, who doesn't notice your presence or you don't even know each other, it is typically a momentary enchantment, a need to fancy a perfect happiness with a romantic hero, and it can be a celebrity actor or a singer, local beauty or, maybe, "forbidden fruit" – your sister's boyfriend.

Should we at all seek the love of that person? First of all, be honest with yourself and ask yourself why you love him. Do you know him enough at all to be able to love him? When we are in such a state of enchantment – ecstasy, we idealize the person. Try to see him in all possible situations in which you haven't seen him yet because you haven't been together: e.g. snoring in his sleep, being at the toilette...

Is he still attractive? Try to be realistic regarding him. I hear many women who cannot stand their husbands' snoring. But when they fall in love with another partner, that same thing doesn't bother them, neither do many more things he does. The woman often wants some man and cries and sighs: "I want him! I love him!" although it is easily discernible that he is not good for her.

"I know that he isn't good for me, but I will die without him. Iris, help!"

I try to explain that it is not good, but as if there is a wall there. Whatever I say is met with a response like: "No, no, I must be with him, I can't live without him." And when the enchantment is gone, what remains is wonder: "I really don't know what it is I saw in that man!"

If you have honestly considered your feelings without imagination and excitement, and found that you really are in love with the man, this prayer before sleep will help you win his love: **"Dear God, if it is good for me, let my message reach him."**

After that, start talking with him: **"My dear..."**, and then speak out his name and surname and then continue: **"I like you very much. I love you!"** Say what you want him to hear from you and about you. At the end, end your message with: **"I am sending you the energy of my love."** The aim is to telepathically send him the message. If he is your soul mate, he will receive it.

Make a love list

If you are lonely and longing for true love, the first step in attracting love into your life can be a love list with the characteristics of your ideal partner, your wishes concerning what you expect from him or her. Although I am encouraging you to do that, be aware this isn't like placing orders after which exactly such a person is going to walk into your life. Such expectations would be a blunder. The love list will be useful only if it serves the purpose of you understanding what kind of partner you really want, which of his characteristics are really most important to you.

You will get an answer if you describe all the desired characteristics of an ideal man or woman in detail and put them on the list.

Characteristics of a man may include, for example, that he is handsome, masculine, tall, impressive, well-groomed, gentle, affectionate, with a sense of humor, well-read, with style and good taste, that he can sing well, play the piano or the guitar, that he is also passionate, imaginative, good lover, but good in the kitchen, too, that he knows how to listen and comfort, successful at work, attached to his family, faithful, that he doesn't grumble, that he is punctual, that he isn't prone to drinking, greed, avarice, selfishness, hypocrisy, jealousy, arrogance... including even the color of his eyes, his profession, bank account, house, income and the type of car he drives.

When men describe their ideal woman, their lists may even include characteristics like: the ideal body measures 90-60-90, blond, brunette, bra size 34, she has to be funny and always in a good mood, faithful in every occasion, attentive mother, good housewife, good cook, prudent with money, careful about her appearances, kind with his friends, nice to his mother and she should love sport. She will rather watch a football match than a soap opera, won't reproach him for coming home late or if he forgets an anniversary, won't expect expensive presents, won't search through his pockets, won't read his mail unless he asks her to...

Put up such a detailed wish list, put a date on it and store it in a box which you can keep somewhere hidden, like at the bottom of your closet or some drawer. Do the same for the following thirty days, without reading what you have already written the previous day, just store the new list in the box. When you have written the thirtieth wish list, take them all out of the box, put them in chronological order and then compare them. Which wish has been written every day? What is it that has changed during the past month? Reviewing your wish list, talk to yourself aloud why some characteristic is important to you. Try to explain what you want and why exactly you want to get it from your beloved.

This way you will learn what really is most important so that you can seek out a partner with such characteristics. Putting up and analyzing love lists is important to make you aware of your need for love so that you can avoid a relationship expecting that your partner will relieve you from economic problems, make you company when you are bored or fill in a void in your life, although you would name such a relationship love, too, but you would be without love in it.

Become your ideal partner

When, with the help of your wish list, you have identified the characteristics you want from your ideal partner, you should yourself behave like your ideal partner towards you – try to make yourself happy. In that state of satisfaction with yourself, you will attract your soul mate, you will be able to give and receive love.

Ask North, South, East and West to send you love

If you are really yearning for a soul mate, for true love which will fulfill you and bring you happiness beyond a superficial short-lived, enamored feeling, which is often rightly called craze, this is a powerful meditation to start off the energy of the Universe to help you.

Every night, or day, if it isn't possible for you to do it at night, look towards the West, East, North, and finally, South, asking aloud every cardinal direction of the world. Start with the West: **"I'm asking the West to carry my voice to my true love to come into my life, here!"** Continue addressing every cardinal point of the world this way. After that, look up, to the sky, and then down at the ground in front of your feet and say: **"My true love is coming here!"** During this address to the Universe, try to be deeply concentrated on your great desire for true love.

Give to receive

Whenever you wish that something beautiful happens to you, first do something good to someone else. Give something to receive something. Do the same when you want love. Give at least the smallest charity donation for the sick and the poor, help somebody in trouble, help in a humanitarian activity, call some telephone number to donate...
However small your contribution or donation may be, it will bring a change in the flow of energy in your life.

Big tidy up

If you want a change in your life, undertake a big tidy up of your home, flat, house. Give or throw away just everything you don't need. That way you will create room for everything new in your living space, for everything that should come, and also for love.

Get rid of negative people

The same way you got rid of old and unnecessary things from your home, which was preventing new things from entering it, get rid of negative people around you. Because of them, there is no room in your life for the new person bringing love. Sever ties with people who underestimate you, judge, criticize and hold you back... Think about every individual in your vicinity. What does s/he fill your emotional space with? How does s/he affect you? It isn't easy to sever such ties, especially if you are a good-hearted and gentle person, and such personalities attract their negative counterparts to feed on them. It is especially difficult if these are your parents, relatives, partner, child...

When you can't simply sever ties with persons who do you wrong, ask higher spheres for help. Imagine the negative person whom you don't want in your life any more, standing in front of you and yourself sending love from your heart into that person's heart. Let that love be like a golden ray of light flowing from you into that person. Then ask: **"God, move this negative person away from me. I want to be in the company of good people only!"**

Meditation for the big tidy up of oneself

Bad relations, many frustrations, negative people and events which have hurt us and piled up into emotional scars prevent us from attracting our soul mate, from realizing true love. Blockages brought about this way must be cleansed from ourselves.

We shall do it by meditations before sleep:

Before you fall asleep, relax completely. Close your eyes, count slowly from ten to one. Imagine yourself in front of a door with a most beautiful sight of marvelous nature behind it. Look at yourself putting your hand on the metal handle and opening the heavy door. Listen to their squeaking. You are entering a beautiful meadow. You are walking through high grass. Savory mottled wildflowers and frisky butterflies are around you. The sky is blue. The sun is shining on you. You are coming to a wonderful miraculous lake. You are putting off your clothes, entering the lake. You are washing your body with water. When you are washed, come out of the lake and raise your head towards the sun. Feel how you are filled with the energy of the sun.

There are large stones arranged in a circle with a big fire in the middle of the circle on the meadow in front of you. You are entering the circle carrying a chest in your hands. Pictures of all negative people who hurt you, all ex partners, all frustrating life situations are in that chest. You are taking pictures one by one, looking at the hurtful person or situation and then throwing them into the flames, one by one, saying: **"I am getting rid of you in my life and throwing you into the fire!"** You are watching it catching fire, burning and disappearing in the fire. You should perform this meditation every day during at least a month.

Changing bad characteristics into good

Honesty towards ourselves is the source of our honesty towards others. Blaming others for our failures, we will get stuck on some wrong path where we shall not be able to progress.

If we want to change our life so that an unhappy life becomes a happy one, there is no other way than to change ourselves. When after a series of unsuccessful relationships we really want to experience true love, we have to openly talk with ourselves about what our previous relationships were like. What is it we would like to repeat, and what would we like to avoid? Let us think about our characteristics which we would like to change, our acts we would like to forget.

There are no people for whom it is easy, since we all tend to blame others for our problems. However, if we want a change, let us start with ourselves. Understand and accept that some of our characteristics and acts also contributed to the bad things which happened to us. Let us hear the wisdom of Mahatma Gandhi who said: **"If you want a change, be that change."** It is a difficult process, but worth the effort.

Here is a meditation which can help you. For example, you admitted yourself that you were extremely jealous. Jealousy will attract a partner who will cheat on you. Since you are constantly distrusting and thus torturing your partner, s/he will do what you are afraid of, even if only out of spite. Therefore, admit that to yourself: **"I am jealous. I**

want to change that." Imagine yourself surrounded with purple flame and beg: **"Change my jealousy into unconditional love and light."**

Do the same with the rest of your characteristics blocking you. This cleanses you from the inside, exchanging the old for the new, the same way you would perform a big tidy up in your home or replace old with new furniture.

Activating feminine energy

I recommend belly dance to women because it activates the feminine energy. Performing these specific dance movements, the woman feels: **"I am perfect. No matter whether I am thin or plump, I am the perfect woman!"**

A woman looking like a million dollar model, but not feeling like a woman, won't find love because a man cannot love a model or a picture, but a woman.

Message to the soul mate

Working on yourself, you become ever more spiritual, and thus more attractive for true love. Through meditation, activate your heart to send the message to your soul mate. The best time for this is in the morning, before getting up, or in the evening, before falling asleep.

First close your eyes, relax and concentrate on your heart. At first just carefully listen to your heartbeats and then imagine it. Watch it in your chest filling with golden light. Imagine the light glowing stronger and pouring out of your heart, projecting out and shining in the whole room like a lighthouse. Having repeated this meditation several times, it will be easy to imagine a picture of yourself shining on the people around you with the light of your heart. Take that light with you wherever you go. Your soul mate will recognize you and approach you.

In the triangle of sunlight

Invoke your soul mate with these words: **"Come to me, my soul mate!"**

Imagine a person of undefined appearance so that you don't recognize who it is, standing in front of you, while the sun is above you. Then imagine a stream of energy from the sun so that the light is on the person representing your soul mate. After that, the stream of energy flows from your soul mate's solar plexus, the central energy chakra between the belly-button and the chest, to your solar plexus and then from you, it flows up to the sun, closing the triangle. Then say: **"I am uniting with my soul mate!"**

You shouldn't invoke your soul mate through this energy if you haven't cleared up your past and your conscience through meditation which has been described in this chapter, for example, in the purple flame. If you are invoking your soul mate from a sore consciousness, there are no prerequisites for the soul mate to come, the same way you can't pour more water into a full glass. You also need to be aware that this way you shouldn't invoke an exact person, even if you are totally convinced s/he is your soul mate. That way you would influence that person's free will, and that is neither allowed, nor is it the path to true love. In case you still do that, you can expect a painful forfeit and a love failure, too. This means that you, from your perspective, can't know who is your soul mate and if you persistently say this meditation thinking of a known person you are in love with, you prevent your soul mate from coming to you.

Letters to the soul mate

You can also write letters to your soul mate, and you will always start them with: **"My dear love..."**

Write about what you have been doing, who you wanted to be with, share something with your soul mate and how you spent one more day expecting your soul mate's coming. Even by thinking about true love, that moment the idea of love will as energy spread throughout the universe, and your soul mate, your true love, will receive the message, no matter where s/he is.

Dream encounters

You often meet your soul mate in your dreams, but later, awake, you generally can't remember that. Still, it is possible to fall asleep and realize an encounter with your soul mate in your dream, even if s/he is dead or very far, or is unknown to you, and to remember the circumstances and the words later. It is true that we need much work on ourselves, we need to raise the frequency of the heart, purify energies and remove blockages to achieve that.

Start with going to sleep at least half an hour earlier than before, so that you don't fall asleep immediately, and every evening, before sleep, say aloud: "I want to be awake in my dream!" Permeate yourself with a feeling of breathing with your whole body, starting with your feet. Breath with your feet, then calves, knees, bones... When you reach the heart, move to your head and after that journey along your body, go back to your heart saying: **"I want to remember my dream! I want to be awake in my sleep!"**

During the day, whenever you have an opportunity, pinch your lower arm and ask yourself: **"Am I awake or dreaming? Yes, I am awake."** Doing this often when you are awake, you will do it in your dream. You will feel the difference, you will become aware that you are dreaming and thus remember your dream.

Such dreams give us hope, not only to encounter our soul mates and the dead whom we are missing, but also to influence what happens while we are awake. Indeed, there are several various levels of consciousness in our dreams which we can reach. The first is that we are aware and that we can remember dreams, the second type is out-of-body experience when we travel through various dimensions, the third, a dream in which we are fully awake and are imagining something we want happening in the future. Such a dream is projected into the future and becomes reality. The fourth type is precognition, the one where we can see the future. However, it is a topic deserving a new book for itself.

Between two worlds

*Between worlds passing.
Hovering between Here and There.
With you I see stars flying,
I know you to the core
In the mystery of my soul.*

*Hanging on your essence,
Crucified between two worlds.
Stepping along endless paths,
Seeking you.*

*Flying from Earth to you
Between two worlds.
Between dreams and reality.*

*My head deep in your bosom,
Your gentle voice calming me,
Helping me to wake up,
Into one more day of reality.*

*Among endless paths,
I am searching for mine,
Path to my home,
Between two worlds.*

Iris Gattegno Tarbuk

Chapter 7

ADVICE FOR WOMEN AFTER FORTY

*My message to older than 40
is that the soul is not measured by years.
For love between two souls
the age of your physical body is not important.
Never, really never, give up on love.*

Old age is a state of mind. Energy of the man and the woman is always young and healthy. It is eternal. What matters is how we are connected with that energy. This is why the age of a body is not an obstacle for love.

There is no more or less beauty in somebody being an older or a younger person, no matter whether it is a man or a woman. Age is not a measure of reality and genuine human essence. Everyone is beautiful to someone.

And it is untrue that the world belongs to the young and that you can have it all when you are young. It is only a pretence originating from the youthful zest of the body, or from the envy of a disappointed and bitter soul in the body of an aged person.

Longing for young body image

Consumer mentality enslaving people today rests on that. Businesses, producing "food supplements" and constantly bombarding us with expensive commercials via the media, in order to sell us *the newest products against aging, cures for all diseases, miraculous preparations for eternal beauty,* are getting richer and richer. I am not talking here about medical care for our physical health, hygiene, medical cosmetics and other stuff contributing to us feeling good in our own skin. I am talking about all those myriads of products where producers promise us *eternal youth* which should be a guarantee for our *eternal happiness*. How lacking and short-sighted! True, the advance of science is slowing down the biological clock, but unfortunately, not even a bit does it influence the prejudice that life happiness and the beauty of living cease to exist when the beauty of our body vanishes. It is also true that physical beauty can be enjoyed, but physical beauty is only short-lived, while true love makes true beauty eternal.

Collective pressure forces women to look according to certain norms. William Shakespeare, a secular and free spirit and an ingenious playwright, free from the doctrine of his era, wrote: "Beauty is in the eye of the beholder." However, our society teaches us that we value beauty according to body curves, hair, eyes, nose, lips... Such evaluation of the beauty is valueless for true love. True love does not depend on what is on the outside.

Preventing aging

When does aging really start? It starts when we give up on ourselves and surrender to aging. Scientists have recently found that human body is created so perfect that it doesn't have to age or die as fast as it happens in today's world. Holy books say that people once lived up to one thousand years, remember Methuselah from the Old Testament. Human body is a biological system, but it is governed by the consciousness of the individual.

Aging is a process which can be slowed down, stopped. Exactly because we always say that the soul is the source of true love, we need to take care of our body health, because the body is the habitat of the soul in this world. Not only by using mental techniques, meditations and prayers, but by physical activity like sport and dance. At the same time, the body and the soul need to be treated with healthy food and generally with healthy and proper life. It is important that you don't do anything just because you feel you have to, but because you love yourself and your body. Listen to your needs. Go out, meet people. God, the Universe and Divine Energy are sending you signals, trust them and follow them. When you are invited somewhere, accept the invitation and see what is awaiting you there.

On the hunt for a man

The older the woman, and especially if she is above 40, and still unmarried, the community looks down on her with growing pity: she doesn't have a husband, nor children, years are passing, she will grow old alone, remain a spinster, and that is shameful. The pressure of the people around – parents, relatives, friends – accumulates: *you have to find someone, you must have children, you must fall in love...*

This is the pressure under which the woman goes hunting a man with whom she will satisfy these societal requirements at any price. And, what happens? The man feels the woman is on the hunt, and he fleets away, retreats, because his instinct is warning him: "She has started hunting me. I shall lose my freedom unless I escape!"

Soft plexus of the older man

Most women in their forties usually search for an older man because he is an easy prey. Their stomach is softer, and it is easier for the *octopus* to enter his solar plexus and reach the desired energy. Indeed, women in such relationships often think they are in love, but it eventually comes down merely to feeding her *octopus*. That is only an exchange of energy, not love.

When I come to some party, I generally see the men, who, in their forties won't even look at women their age, let alone at those older than they are. One of my friends went to a disco club and tested how men reacted to her age. She told some of them that she was 48, and some that she was 39. Their reactions to this same person were completely different.

If they thought she was below 40, she was interesting for further conversation and if they thought she was 48, they ignored her. Due to such reactions, women often conceal their age and it is fully morally justified regarding the hypocrisy of societal standards.

It can sometimes even be practical to start a relationship with such a lie and it can even be useful, because this "small white lie" is used to outwit a prejudice. It isn't a game where fair-play applies, anyway.

The truth is that many men conceal their years, too, because they don't want to be the victims of prejudice.

Still, the society is much more benevolent towards them, and there is even a saying: "Men are like wine. The older, the better!"

The source of youth in a younger woman

An average man above forty is typically interested only in younger women. The marriage of the 73-year-old rock-granny Tina Turner with her 17 years younger fiancée is an exception even in the world of rock' n' roll.

We are talking about the average man who is on the hunt for a younger woman and doesn't think at all how fatal it could be for him, because, as a rule, he won't know how to deal with her strong sexual energy. She is attracting him as a fountain of youth, and he doesn't know that the girl or the young woman has a strong *octopus* which will feed on him until he falls totally exhausted. Even if he senses something, he doesn't want to know anything about it.

A young woman, besides the source of energy she desires, seeks fatherly support, sponsorship and protection from an older man. In their relationship he is happy because he believes she gives him youth. He will feel younger with her, and won't even notice that she is twisting him around her little finger till she drains and totally dismisses him. The man left so, grows rapidly old, crumples down more than it might be expected regarding his chronological age. And the young beauty, empowered with this winning, searches for a new source of sexual energy and sponsorship.

Sometimes true love develops from such a relationship between an older man and a younger women, and then they both achieve completion through their relationship, and both fill with energy making love. Still, it is generally mostly a business exchange of the type: *quid pro quo*.

Women faster to reach the heart frequency

Apart from seeing young women as sources of his eternal youth, the older man is also well disposed towards them because he considers them to be *less complicated* than women of his age.

In the sense of energy, women achieve the frequency of the heart faster than men. However, the majority does not achieve that because they intended so, but because after their 40, their *octopus* weakens and stops functioning as their main driver. An older woman, with a tired *octopus*, competing with the stronger energy of a younger woman, does not succeed in catching a man. At that age, she is either still unsuccessfully trying with her *octopus*, or raises her body to the level of heart frequency and lets it guide her. When it happens, the woman sends different signals, unfortunately of the kind a small number of men can recognize. As previously said – in their early childhood men are taught not to react to a woman's heart but to her *octopus*.

This is why at that age there are many women who are alone and lonely, while men who are their age are in relationships.

Free in love with a younger man

Women above 40 sometimes like to show that they don't need anybody and they send the message to the world around them: **"I am successful and happy alone with myself."** This is how they actually give up on their need for love.

My message to women above 40:

The fact is that one can't count years of the soul and the years of your body don't matter in true love. If a woman of 40 falls in love with a man of 20 and if he loves her in return, what is the problem? Love and be loved freely, it is your right, it is true love, and people can say whatever they want.

However, for a woman of 40 to be able to enjoy free love, it is necessary that she stops judging other people, because as we judge others, they judge us the same. The moment we are out of the collective pressure to judge and evaluate, life becomes easier. We don't judge others, they don't judge us, we don't judge ourselves. It is the path to freedom.

Our modern life, unfortunately, isn't much associated with the spiritual. Now and here we are to develop, grow and step out of our circle, to improve our existence. We live unconscious that we are all in one matrix, and our task is to try to open our eyes and be aware of our existence. So, if somebody makes us happy, why should we care what others think about it.

Start by loving yourself

Loving yourself is more important than anything. You will achieve this by changing your perspective on the world and people: wherever you go and whoever you meet, find something good and nice, something wonderful, something delightful in them.

When we see the beauty in others, in time we will start seeing the beauty in ourselves.

It is very important to compliment ourselves. Stop searching for bad things on and in yourself and what you did wrong, and start noticing the good. Congratulate yourself every time you do something good.

Take care of your energy

It is important to afford yourself at least five minutes of meditation per day to increase your energy. If you have an appropriate prayer which, within your faith, helps you to do that – pray.

If you meditate, note that the same meditation is not appropriate for everybody. Some women will meditate passively, deep in their inspiring thoughts and visions, while others will do that walking, touring the countryside, doing something they like, dancing, working out...

I also recommend that you find yourself a good bioenergy expert and visit him/her regularly the same way you regularly visit your dentist or leave your car at the mechanic: let the expert examine your energy body, cleanse and fill it in... Massage will also help. Regardless of the sort, a massage moves and renews energies, and the body requires attention and tenderness, especially in the people suffering due to a lack of love. This way we learn to pay attention to ourselves, to do something for ourselves. Exercises like yoga, tai chi, falun gong, are good to energize us, and dancing is always good, too...

However, walking is most important. Especially if you are very unhappy, even depressed. Force yourself to walk. Going to the countryside is a must. Besides forests, where there are many trees filling us with energy, the sea, rocks and crystals also make a wonderful impact.

I meditate walking in the woods. While walking, I close my eyes and feel the energy growing in my body. That wave of energy goes from the lower parts of my body upwards and every particle of my body is filled with energy.

Filling with energy will especially help women who have problems of overweight. Indeed, one of the causes of gaining undesired kilograms in women older than 40 is giving up on love. And when you give up on love, and I don't mean only romantic love, you are hungry all the time and you eat all the time, but you are hungry again. That is a hunger which can't be stopped nor controlled; shuffling food in unsuccessful attempts to fill the vast emptiness and to punish yourselves, at the same time sending around the message: "I'm not happy!" Instead of doing it with food, fill yourself with energy.

Some men are bothered by the same problem, and I recommend that they also fill themselves with energy instead of doing it with food.

Sing to your love

Create a song to your love and sing it wholeheartedly. Let both the music and the text be yours and sing in the bathtub, while you are cooking, walking, whenever it suits you. Try to get out of the limitations of collective fears and prejudice that you won't find love after you are 40. Believe that it is possible and love will come. No matter how old you are, don't restrain yourself in this belief.

Overcome bitterness and depression

Work on yourself, love yourself. If you find yourself feeling bitter, angry, disappointed, despondent, suspicious... resist and overcome it. Accept all means to fight despondency. Meditate, fill with light and rise to the frequency of the heart because there are others whom you have to meet at that frequency. If a prayer helps, then – pray.

First date? See the man through your heart

Don't hesitate to meet an unknown man, whether the meeting has been arranged by friends, via ads or the Internet. Make it an opportunity to practice observing from your heart on the person you have met for the first time. Do not miss the chance, it may literally be the love of your life...

Observing from the heart means that you don't bother if the man is 40, 50 or 60, if he is educated, well-off, if he has a career... but how you are feeling in his company, if your rhythms and music are in harmony, if you can see the light shining on you and on him.

The moment you switch on your brain, you switch on criticism and switch off any chance for love: "He is 60, he can have a heart attack during sex, he is short, bald..." These are not the thoughts which will bring your two souls to touch.

Therefore, when you meet someone, close your eyes for a moment and ask your heart for the opinion on that person. Any feelings? Is his energy pleasing you, are you feeling contented, peaceful, relaxed? When you start doing so, you will soon see the soul of the man you are with, and not his face, build... If you really want love, practice observing from the heart, strengthen your intuition and listen to it.

Never give up on love

I repeat this message to women above 40:

Do not fall victims of the fear imposed on you by your milieu (parents, relatives, friends and acquaintances), the fear that your world and you with it are going under because you are aging. Love of two souls doesn't mind the age of the physical body.

Do not panic, devote yourself to attracting your soul mate, finding true love, like I described in the previous chapter. Never, ever give up on love!

Chapter 8

SUSTAINING LOVE IN A RELATIONSHIP AND MARRIAGE

Every seed of love needs to be nourished, watered and cherished like a brittle plant. Even if the two who are in love or married
aren't soul mates, but there is still mutual respect after the magic of sex has vanished,
love can grow and flourish between them.

Love is wonderful, it is pure joy, but if you aren't working on yourself and not nourishing it, love can eventually turn into suffering. We often extend that suffering because we are simply of the kind that likes to suffer.

Love can be compared with an elevator which you enter to climb a higher floor, rise to a higher ground. I

f you know where you want to go, and if you press the right button, then you go up, where you want. If you don't know where you want to go, you are stuck. When you are stuck, you become claustrophobic, overwhelmed with fear growing into panic.

Survival of the seed of love

If you look into the life of an average family, you won't see a great deal of love there. The husband and the wife work, coming home nervous, children are at school coping constantly in competition with other children, while nobody teaches them how to achieve love relationships. Parents blame each other, prove whose guilt is bigger in everyday problems brought by life, especially at times of crisis. And there always is a crisis, if nowhere else, then in relationships... This is exactly that negative energy which destroys love in the family and the family itself.

Indeed, love needs to be cherished. Every seed of love needs to be nourished and watered and then love between two people will grow and survive even if they aren't soul mates, even if they have not married in true love, even when an *octopus* witnessed their holy vows. Even there a small seed from which love can grow can be found, only if after the disappearance of the magic of sex there remained a seed of mutual respect. Love is always worthwhile investing and that is why it is necessary to find time for love.

Ten minute talk with your partner alone

Partners need to talk with each other alone at least ten minutes a day. The topic of that talk doesn't matter, it is unimportant. If your days have a very busy schedule, try to go to bed ten minutes earlier and talk before sleeping.

Talk with each other about ordinary, everyday topics, about your day, remember some happy moments you had together, some happy events you experienced together, talk about what is bothering you, talk about and solve some problem together, introduce your wife or your husband into your world little by little.

Look each other in the eye

Eyes are the mirror of your soul. Open eyes – open soul. People who are hiding something avert their eyes or wear sunglasses even when there is no sun. We say that they have guilty conscience, their soul is unclean. That is the main reason why today people avoid looking each other in the eye. However, partners bound by love which they value and who don't have any hidden agendas towards each other, but want to be happy together, really don't have an excuse not to look each other in the eye.

I recommend partners to search for themselves in the eye of each other, because it is how their souls meet. If you don't have such spontaneous opportunities, agree on the time when each day you will sit at the table opposite each other, hold hands and look each other in the eye for at least five minutes.

Talk about problems

If something in your partner bothers you, don't hold it back, and under no circumstances should you complain about the problem to your male and female friends before the two of you have discussed it.

If you are unhappy in your marriage, don't let yourself be a victim. Marriage isn't a prison, but an expression of two people's free will. Respect yourself, do not give anybody nor anything the power to undermine your self-respect and to set boundaries to your free will.

Before you decide to separate, ask yourself: **"Why are we together? Why did I fall in love with him? Why did I propose to her?"** If you still can remember why, if you still can evoke that feeling, try to enhance it. If you don't manage to do it alone, ask a psychologist, marriage counselor or your spiritual advisor for help.

How to strengthen faded love

When you wake up in the morning, before you devote yourself to something else, close your eyes and imagine looking into your heart. Fill it with the color of gold, the symbol of love energy and watch the stronger and stronger golden light emanating from your heart after that. With your heart filled so, look at your husband or wife lying in bed next to you and think: **"This is my wife. I love her!", "This is my husband. I love him!"** This way you can stir up your disheartened love and bring soul into life with your partner when it becomes boring.

Take an inventory of yourself

Once a week ask yourself questions which are bothering you in your relationship, note them down in a notebook and try to answer them honestly:

Do I really love my partner?

What is it I expect from my partner?

What do I miss in my partner?

Why am I not happy?

What can I do to be happy?

What is it I expect s/he should do to make me happy?

Is there something in me triggering bad things in our relationship?

Do I have what to talk about with him?

If we can't go on building what we had, can we build something new?

Is there passion left between us?

If there is no more passion, can I bring it back into our relationship?

If he cheated on me, had I somehow contributed?

If s/he cheated on me, can I forgive him/her?

If I can't forgive him/her and go on with life without reproaching, should we continue to live together or should we go our own separate ways?

These questions need to be written and you need to think deeply about answers. Devote as much time as you need to find the answers. Thus you will gradually understand what you are missing, what you can and what you need to do. You will see that there are many things you can change and many ways to upgrade your love and improve your marriage.

Union of the free and the honest

Marriage and partner relationship should be a union of free and honest people. It is fatal if partner relationships rest on lies and double-facedness. Those lying to their spouses and partners, who don't openly say with whom they go somewhere and what they will do there, are making a big mistake. Be responsible and honest towards yourselves and towards your partner. Go where you want, do what you want! And say it openly.

Why should we lie? Your partner should accept you for who you are. It is clear where such behavior comes from. We are slaves to the perception that we need to pamper our partner to make him/her stay with us and love us. That is a fatal consequence of the wrong model of child upbringing where parents taught us that they loved us only when we obeyed. Indeed, many people are unhappy in their married life because they expect to get love only when they obey.

Without lies and cover-ups

I have a friend who is very successful, wonderful, intellectually strong... She wants love, seeks a soul mate, but she worries in advance and asks me: "I love to paint. What if my future husband doesn't like it?" The answer is clear: "Then he isn't the man for you."

To be in a relationship and marriage doesn't mean losing yourself, but having one person with whom we are going to develop and grow.

There is no place for lies in a marriage. Even when the husband or the wife want to be with somebody else, it has to be said. It will hurt both, but it offers a possibility of choice: we either see we have problems and start solving them, or get a divorce. Fidelity to only one partner is a concession we are making to the culture we live in. If we have agreed and our partner expects that, we should only be with him/her. Marriage infidelity is acceptable in some cultures. For example, among some Indian tribes all are on good terms although they exchange their partners every evening. It isn't a source of conflict between them, nor is there competition. Freedom of choice is accepted and respected.

Meditation to strengthen the relationship

Awareness that you are with your partner at your own free choice can be strengthened with this meditation:

Close your eyes, relax and imagine that you can see the inside of your body. Starting from your feet, visualize slowly each of your organs, every bone, every part of your body. Fill them with a lot of energy, lighten them with golden rays. Peacefully enjoy in that inner light of yours and say: **"This here is me, married at my own free will. My husband is with me at his own free will. We want to be together."** When you accept this, your marriage will be much better.

Meditation to reconcile

Arguing with our partner, but with any other person too, we are losing the power and energy. We shall return it through a meditation I recommend that you should perform when you are in some conflict. We invoke the person who hurt us: **"Come to me!"** Then we imagine that person standing in front of us and we say: **"Give me back my energy which you took."** After that we watch the energy looking like golden rays of light flowing from that person's solar plexus towards our solar plexus, and we say: **"Give me energy!"** We take that energy, thank and return the energy sending rays into his/her solar plexus saying: **"I am returning the energy I took, I forgive you with love and light."**

S/he returned energy to us, we returned energy to her/him, nobody is at loss and nobody is considered to be guilty nor indebted. Reconciliation.

I will reveal a little secret of my marriage. I do this meditation after every fight with my husband. When he comes back home after that, there is a flow of pure energy of peace and love between us.

Fear of being abandoned

"I'm happy and content with him. Everything makes sense with him."

"I can't imagine a day, let alone my life without her."

A woman in love never knows how to overcome the fear that the man she loves will abandon her and that love will vanish like a soap bubble. Men in love suffer the same way. It's only human.

When you love, you are connected with your spiritual self, with the Divine Energy, you are permeated with well-being, harmony. Actually, you aren't so much afraid that your partner will leave you, but that the energy, the state of your spirit, will disappear. Your partner is only a reminder that such a state of your soul exists, and we sometimes say: **"I am in love with love."**

Therefore, when you are in love, take the advantage of it, try to sustain that frequency and that sort of energy so that you always have that feeling of being connected with God, regardless of whether your partner is there or not.

One step before divorce

After some crisis, your marriage either becomes wonderful and stronger, or you divorce. Spouses are often unaware why their marriage is in crisis, and so they can't save it. This is why communication between partners is necessary in the first place, but after an open talk and insight in ourselves and answering the question why we aren't happy in our marriage, we will reach something related to us. At that moment we won't be obsessed with our partner any more, but will turn to ourselves. Your spouse with whom you are in conflict has only served as a tool to show you where you got stuck. When you are aware of that, you will decide whether you will solve the issue and remain in that marriage. If you don't want that, say: **"Thank you for the experience. I'm getting on with my life!"**

When your baby transforms paradise into hell

Some people have been married for a long time when they see that they actually don't know, that they have never known their partner. They had some idea of what they had wanted their spouse to be, and it seems that didn't have much to do with reality. Sometimes one partner really loves the other, would do anything for him/her, but love requires two of them. If only one of them loves, there is no happiness in it.

A young mother has recently told me, her eyes full of tears, that her marriage has been falling apart after she and her husband finally realised the dream of their life. They had spent four years in various treatments and therapies to get pregnant. And when she finally got pregnant, paradise turned into hell. Instead of caring and nurturing her during her pregnancy, her husband started abusing her. As if he had got mad. He shouted at her, grumbled all the time, came home later and later... This woman is completely confused, because, as she puts it, they don't have any problems. They have been in love since their high school, both graduated, have good jobs, they are financially stable, their extended families get along well, and the only thing missing in that paradise was a child. When it was conceived, their world shattered. In this concrete case, the main binding connection between the spouses disappeared. What kept them tightly united – their wish to have a child – has now vanished. They don't have what to talk about any more. The truth about their relationship has started emerging.

It isn't rare for a woman who had a wonderful marriage, to lose her husband because he found another woman while the former was in hospital for special monitoring and care during pregnancy. This means that there has never been true love between them, but only an illusion of love.

If something like this happens to you, let him go. Your husband isn't your possession, neither are you his. Marriage isn't a prison with no exit. If he doesn't love you and doesn't want to be with you, then he isn't for you. You have acquired the life experience you should have acquired with him, learn from it, overcome your constraints and get on. Why should you turn your life into suffering?

Divorce with love

Although I advise women not to struggle to keep their husband if he wants to leave them, there aren't many who can and want to follow that advice. They mostly come for advice how to keep him.

I tell them: **"Go deep into your innermost parts and look for the answer if you really love him or you only want to own him. If you love him, and know that he is happy when he isn't with you, let him be happy."**

Let us be honest to ourselves. It is a fact that we are scared of divorce mostly because of money and ownership. I am certain that, if we all had much money, many couples would be divorced. If there are children from that marriage, it is better for them, too, if their parents are divorced than if they are witnessing constant fighting and thrashing at home.

If you are divorcing, your farewell should be beautiful, with love. Tell your partner: **"I'm giving you your freedom. With my love. move on with you life."** *Forgive without blackmailing*

If you are persistent in your love and you want to keep him, first you have to be prepared to forgive him everything. Mutual life can be built only on complete forgiveness. Sometimes men or women who have cheated leave their partner for good, not even trying to continue with their marriage because they are convinced that their partner will never forgive them, and that their life will be miserable. Therefore, first ask yourself: "Can I forgive and truly forget?" It is worth fighting for, only if the answer is positive.

Striving to keep your partner, must under no circumstances be blackmailing, especially not with children or property, or, which is also horrible, by blaming your partner for your sickness, e.g. a heart stroke with these words: **"See what you have done to me! I am terribly sick because of you. If you leave, I shall die, and you will answer to our children because you will be guilty for them not having their mother!"**

Meditation for your marriage revival

Regardless of the reason why your partner wants to leave you, this meditation will help you to revive and strengthen your marriage: **"Give me back my energy which you took"** described in the part on fighting and reconciliation. Ask from your partner to give you back your strength: **"Give me energy!"** and then return it to him with love.

Fight for your partner working on yourself – your goodness, cleansing negative energy, awakening your heart, your energy of love. Ask yourself: **"What is it in me that I created such a marital situation that s/he behaves like that?"** Change it. Don't be one of those people who spend their life blaming others for their problems, stuck there forever and never moving on.

Help him/her pack up

It is difficult to admit that we are the causative agent of our problems. But accept it as a challenge, as an opportunity to grow spiritually, develop as a person. Thoroughly explore why you haven't been happy in the relationship so that you forced your partner to do something like that to you. Maybe you need to be miserable. Maybe you live the scenario: **"I have no luck. I don't care about anything."** When your partner cheats on you with another person, you get a confirmation for the condition: **"I'm the victim! Nobody loves me!"** You will sometimes find the cause of the problem in completely profane things – for example, there isn't enough sex in your marriage, or you don't cook good enough or you don't have enough money. Well, if your partner wants to leave you for these reasons, help him/her pack up. Such a partner should leave as soon as possible.

Should you take back a partner who has left you?

Ask yourself why you want your partner back. If it is because of your ego, or competing with the person who *took* him, your hurt vanity or desperation because you believe it is an indicator showing that you aren't attractive and beautiful any more; none of these are real reasons to strive for your partner's return to you. For example, men generally leave with much younger women and it hurts their wives' self-esteem.

If that has happened to you and if reading this book you have realized that he was grabbed by a woman with a strong *octopus*, you may reckon: **"I know this won't last. She will consummate and exhaust**

him, and when she dumps him, I will be waiting here, I will forgive him."

Well, then wait. If it is your conscious choice, I understand that. Still, in most cases, it is a poor choice.

Men typically don't come back. And most often it is for the best.

Why husbands cheat

Why do husbands get involved in adultery? In most cases it is because another woman with a strong *octopus* caught your husband at a moment when he was weak and when your marriage was loaded with negative energy. People who can't stand you, who wish you wrong, have a big role in that, and that negative energy sabotages the relationship between you and your husband.

In that case you need to fight for your husband in a spiritual way. Go to a spiritual advisor, cleanse that negative energy and its influence on you as a couple, pray, cleanse your energy and blockage with meditation, raise your love energy, go to a spiritual revival, pray to God to bring your love back to you.

How to bring him back

A song which you write yourself for your love will help. Sing it aloud every night before you fall asleep. Make that song a part of your feelings. Sing as if you know that trees, stones, the East, the West, wind, water... are listening and that they will convey it through the whole Universe.

It is important that you sing to love in general, and not only to the partner who has left you. If he is your true love, he will come back. If he isn't, you will attract new, true love with your song.

Don't force him to stay

Here is a case which is an obvious example of that. A husband and father of two young children, in a young, but unstable marriage, was caught by a woman with a strong *octopus*. She subdued him so much that he completely neglected his family and work because of her. He was fired from work, because, instead of doing his job, he talked with her on the mobile phone for hours. His wife suspected that he was cheating on her, but everything came to daylight when her rival's husband appeared at her doorstep – asking her to get control of her husband.

She pleaded him and fought with him, but nothing helped. Her husband didn't want to give up his lover, yet his wife didn't give up on him, and still, her only wish was to keep him. Soon her husband was injured in a car accident, so that, due to his pelvis concussion he couldn't get out of bed for months, not even to go to the toilette. His lover quited her relationship with him and immediately found a new lover, and his wife finally had him only for herself – she bathed him, fed him, changed his diapers... But for what good? He didn't stay with her of his own free will. The moment he is back on his feet, he will leave.

Sometimes a woman who has been cheated on and left by her husband feels a need to hurt someone and she seduces some married man to inflict his wife the pain and suffering she had experienced herself.

It can bring only a short relief, because you won't achieve happiness by making other people unhappy.

From love to hate

Departure of her husband was naturally difficult to accept to a woman who had been with him from childhood. They grew up together. They fell in love as 15-year-olds. They were always together, and married after graduation. They started developing a business. She got pregnant. While she was at home lying in bed and guarding her pregnancy, her husband was attracted to one of their female employees. He left the woman with whom he had spent more than a half of his life. He left without even coming to see his newborn daughter. They divorced and divided property. He transferred his property into the ownership of his new wife and reported himself as unemployed in order not to pay child support for his daughter. He never called nor did he ever visit her.

This abandoned woman has been trying to get the child support at the court. But she can't. He keeps coming to the court in an Armani suit and hand made Italian shoes, but he also claims that he doesn't have income and can't give a dime for his child. That woman suffers even more because he hurt their daughter. How is it possible that an innocent love turns into such acts of humiliation and hatred. How and where has love gone?

That has never been true love, but youth infatuation. The moment there appeared real life difficulties – complicated pregnancy, child, business – the husband fell a victim of the first strong *octopus*. And the new wife imposed her regime on him ultimately: "I don't want to know anything about your earlier life, she got her half, break up with everything from your past, devote yourself only to me and to your new family."

Recovery after separation

On our way of recovery after love has definitely died or after divorce, we should rely on a belief that God, Higher Consciousness, Universal Force is leading us through life, and, even if at that moment we don't understand why, that what happened was exactly the best for us, and that future is bringing something much better for us.

When the person we love leaves us, we are desperate, our soul hurts, we shed tears, cry inconsolably and talk to friends to relieve the pain. And when we recover a bit from the shock, we ask ourselves: Why did he leave me? What could I have done to change it? What in me caused that my partner wished to leave me? What would my life look like had we remained together?

Sometimes, after tears, we understand that separation was the best solution for us. One woman shed tears for months over a man who left her until she heard he had got married again, but that he wasn't happy. He cheated on his new wife, battered her, abused her. The woman stopped crying having understood that it was god she got rid of him. Had he come back or had they remained together, her life would have been like that new wife's.

Cleansed we welcome true love

However much your separation may be hurting, even if in that pain you swore that you would never again let anyone hurt you, never give up on love. Repeat to yourself, hundreds of times if necessary: "I'm not giving up on love! I will never give up on love!" Because the love that left, the one who left you, wasn't your soul mate, there was no true love between you. That is useful too – bad experience will cleanse you and it is time you start searching for your soul mate, for true love – at the level of the heart.

Should you confess adultery?

I've been asked whether it is advisable to confess our husband or wife that we cheated on them, or it is better not to say anything and protect them from the pain and disappointment. My answer is that, in any case, you should confess the adultery. If your relationship is true love, your partner will forgive you, it will enhance your relationship. If it isn't, you will break up and get on. If you continue living with that lie, the lie will strain you destroying both you and your relationship in which you remained concealing your adultery.

Admit your adultery in some nice way. Choose some appropriate occasion, when the knowledge of your adultery will least hurt your partner, when you estimate that it could even enhance your relationship, since you will put the vanity of the body (if that is what it was) and your momentary weakness into the perspective of the full and rich relationship of your true love. View what happened as an opportunity to make your marriage better.

Ask for forgiveness, and the other party should forgive – not for the preservation of the marriage, but for yourselves.

How love vanishes

I so often hear people sobbing: **"We were so much in love, and we had it so wonderful, but now it seems the whole thing was a lie? Where has love disappeared?"**

You have to understand and accept that everybody has his/her own life path. Sometimes these life paths are mutual, we go along them close together, but at one moment we take different directions. Everyone has hard time accepting that his/her partner has taken his own path. We have our vision and we want our partner in it.

If your partner took his own, different path, that doesn't mean there hadn't been love between you, or that love isn't going to be between you again. If it wasn't love for life, that doesn't mean the love wasn't real. At that moment of your life, it was the best, and it was real. As a child, you wear shoes size 30, and when you grow up, you need size 40. Shoes size 40 may be the right size, but if your feet are 30, you need to wait to grow up so that 40 fits.

Buying love with sacrifice

Everybody, especially women, need to become aware of one big truth of life: Love isn't bought with sacrifice! Although there are men who so behave, women are those who, due to their upbringing more often accept the imposed attitude that they deserve love only if they make sacrifice, only if they abstain from their own wishes, needs and interests. Then, at one time of their life, they understand that none of those to whom they showed their love that way, sacrificed back, that they aren't really loved, and they conclude that all their sacrifice was in vain.

If you want to experience true love, you have to change such an attitude and understand and accept that you need your loved ones exclusively for yourself, for who you are, and not for what you give. It is crucial that you get rid of your prejudice still existing in many societies and religions, that marriage isn't an unbreakable sanctity and that it has to be preserved at any cost, that the woman has to suffer literally anything – even if her husband deprecates her, harasses, cheats, batters, abuses her. If you don't feel well in your marriage – get a divorce.

Chapter 9

SPECIAL ADVICE FOR MEN

Although this chapter is nominally intended for men, it is clear that it is especially important that women read it, since it can help in understanding and preserving the relationship and marriage

When a man is in love with a woman, she can ask and get anything she wants from him. Some women will take the best from men and realise true love with them. Some will drive them crazy, take advantage, discard, take everything from them, but it isn't love. It is sexual manipulation. This is why I primarily advise men that they shouldn't be afraid and ashamed to love, that they should relax and enjoy it, but in such a way that they don't let the women they love to manipulate them.

Say "I love you!" as often as possible

Contrary to deeply ingrained prejudice, men can feel romantic love. However, since the man mostly learned from his mother that her love is a reward when he had been good or obedient, he finds it easiest to express his love for a woman by buying something and giving it to her as a gift.

Of course, it is nice to give your beloved a gift, but the woman who loves you only needs tenderness and a hug and the three words: **"I love you!"**

First love

His first love is crucial for the love happiness of a man. Indeed, young men, teenagers and 20-year olds are amorous, romantic, but sensitive, too. Their hearts are pure and open and that is the reason why it is easy to hurt them. It is easy to manipulate them and women take advantage of that.

After their first love, many are so much hurt that, getting older, their heart is shutting down. They defend themselves from being manipulated and disappointed again with sex. They remain in a sex relationship where they believe that they, and not the woman, are in control.

An average man can become bitter and selfish especially after his 40, while powerful men become cold and rigid. Such men use their masculine energy exclusively for sex and crave for youth and a beautiful body in women.

Of course, it is all a delusion and self-deceit, because craving true love, and not sex, none of them is happy in themselves. His male pride prevents him from admitting it to himself, but through young women he is trying to experience the feeling of his first love when he was a young man with pure heart, vulnerable. Many were hurt as young shutting down their hearts after that, and have never experienced true love, thus growing into bitter and unhappy adult men.

Pride and romance

I am addressing young men with this message:

Don't ever allow anybody to shut your heart down. If a woman wasn't nice to you – she isn't the only woman in this world. You should know that there are others who will relate to you with love and care, who will respect and love you. You should know that among women there is your soul mate with whom you can experience full and eternal love happiness.

For that you have to nurture your romantic side, although many will often call it female. Nurture your male personality, engage in football, boxing, wrestling or whatever sport you like, drink beer, play cards in the male company... But watch romantic movies, read love stories, enjoy romantic music, also.

Power of the heart

How can a man protect himself from women who have a strong *octopus* and whose aim is not love but possession? You can do it only with your heart.

Learn how to see with your heart. When you feel lost in sexual desire for a woman, think about your heart, fill it with light and see that woman's soul through your heart. What is her soul like? What do you feel for her? What does she feel for you.

A man who wants to attract a woman who is his soul mate, can do it only by working on the frequency of his heart. He shouldn't hide his emotions and he shouldn't avoid telling the woman: "I love you!"

He shouldn't think about who utters these words first – if it was him or her. It isn't important. When you feel love and wish to express it to the woman you love, say it.

Relationship with your mother

How can you put the relationships with your mother in order? Parents should be respected at all times, but your own family should be of supreme importance to you. There shouldn't be competition between your mum and your wife. Under no circumstances should you allow that. A man who can't be happy with his wife because of his relationship with his mother, can't be happy.

For both the man and the woman, final message to reach happiness and love is:

Open yourself to spirituality – either through religion, meditation, or some other way. Spirituality is of utmost importance.

Chapter 10

HOMOSEXUAL LOVE

When we see love as energy
it has no precursors.
It is neither heterosexual nor it is homosexual.
Love is love.

Those who exclude homosexuals have a completely wrong concept of love. They view love primarily as a sexual relationship, and sex is only an addition to love. When we are completely free, we choose and have a diversity of love and sex. We can have sex without love, love without sex, and love with sex.

There are cases when a man deeply loves another man, but doesn't feel like having sex with him. There are cases when a man feels like having sex with another man, being in love with a woman at the same time. And, there are cases when a man loves another man, or when a woman loves another woman, wanting to have both a sexual relationship and a life together.

However someone may like it or not, there have always been homosexual people and they have equal human rights like everybody else to be happy and love.

Throughout history, homosexuals were ostracized, prosecuted, attacked, even killed, for example during the inquisition and nazism. It seems difficult to accept that love is love, and that it can be true when someone is gay. Only God knows, while no people do, why someone is more inclined to the same sex.

I feel very sad to see how some people persistently fight against homosexuals instead of fighting for love in their own lives. They waste much energy against the people whom they don't understand, while at the same time they are alienating themselves from love. You can't have love in your life while you are fighting against love in other people's lives.

Disastrous concealment

I shall only ask a few practical questions ensuing from my experience as a spiritual guide, from my encounters with people and knowledge of their life situations:

What is better for parents: discard their son because he loves a man, discard their daughter because she loves a woman, or support them in their happiness? Is it better for a homosexual person to marry a person of the opposite sex because of the societal pressure, to start a family, to have children and let everything turn into a difficult life drama and break up when his/her true nature emerges?

One man, being in the bedroom with his lover, was caught *in flagranti* by his wife who came home from work earlier. She was so smitten by what she saw, it shattered everything she considered to be the basis of her happy family, that she committed suicide, leaving two small children motherless.

Another woman, finding out that her husband was a homosexual and that he had been cheating on her, became promiscuous. She didn't divorce him, since they had children, but she felt very guilty. She believed that she wasn't feminine enough and that it pushed him into looking for sexual satisfaction in the embrace of men. Proving that she was attractive, she became promiscuous, having sex with everybody who showed a bit of interest in her. She suffered for that, and her husband also suffered, because he felt guilty for her trouble. She started hating him.

Wouldn't it be better if these men freely realized their nature?

Not gay, but in a homosexual relationship

There has lately emerged a process opposite to denying one's heterosexual orientation. Society has become liberal, homosexual love has been accepted in a growing number of countries, while at the same time relationships between men and women are becoming ever more complicated. I see men who turn to homosexual relationships although they aren't gay. They choose that because it is easier for them to live together with another man.

The woman of today is strong, decisive, dangerous. Old relationships when men were hunters and women cared for home are disappearing. Men and women live similar lives. Women work like men, they fight in the army, wear police uniforms, fly in space. The division between them in public and in private life is disappearing. Today's woman doesn't need a man to get a child. When she feels the call of nature, she goes to the sperm bank for that.

So it is more and more difficult for a man to be in a relationship with a woman, and it's easier to be with a man with whom he will develop a relationship of brotherly understanding and agreement. The man doesn't need a woman any more to have a child. A growing number of countries allows surrogate pregnancies, and homosexual couples can adopt children.

I'm very sad that so many people are forced to live in hiding. Both those who don't dare admit that they are homosexual, and those who don't dare live heterosexually.

Universal love problems

We all need to raise our love energy to the frequency of the heart and then, from there, solve all open issues of our existence, search for our partner and our love, our touch with eternity and God through a relationship in accordance with our genuine nature.

Homosexual couples are bothered by the same problems like the heterosexual ones. Insecurity, fear of losing the loved one, jealousy, adultery are present there, too, and some are also curious and would like to try how they would feel in a heterosexual relationship.

I had an opportunity to see love so pure and beautiful between two men, that there was no doubt – it was real, unconditional love. That is why I say it isn't important who you love. Embrace that happiness and the feeling. The important thing is that you love.

Love without fear

All meditations for finding true love and attracting your soul mate in this book are meant for the people with the same sex orientation, too. They help them as they help others, to accept their love, to love without being forced to do so, and without doubts. These are more difficult to achieve for homosexuals when they aren't sure if they are gay, or when they aren't really happy with their sexual orientation.

The following meditation will help them to freely accept that they are gay:

Close your eyes, relax completely. Imagine looking at your heart, which is filling with love energy and radiating golden light, and say:

"I am in love with being in love. I am in love with my partner. I am happy in that love energy and because I don't let fear intrude our love."

If you aren't sure which sex attracts you

To those who aren't sure whether they are homosexual or heterosexual, in their search for true love, I recommend all meditations and techniques to attract their soul mates as already described in this book. The difference is that when you visualize your soul mate, you shouldn't define his/her sex. Imagine a human shape without sex or other determinants. When you are making your wish list, you should write:

"I expect my love, of whatever sex, to be..."

Afterword

Iris is one of the most extraordinary persons I have met in the 30 years of my career as a journalist. I personally know many people whom she helped and really miraculously influenced their lives. That was the exact reason why I suggested that her advice should be available to the wider public in a book form.

Since the last interview with her for the exclusive issue of Corps Diplomatique magazine for the international business community in Croatia, we hadn't met for several years, but when I called her with a proposal that we could write a book together, not a bit surprised by my call, Iris immediately accepted the idea.

When we met, soon after that, in her first sentence she informed me that through her meditation she received an answer that I was the person with whom she should write her book and that we were meant to make a big success with it. All the bigger for her, since as a young girl she put it on the second place on her wish list, the first being helping people. And now it was the right time to do it.

I talked with Iris many times, partly in Croatian, mostly in English, even with some Hebrew words. Putting together her flows of thoughts from meditations and merging into *akasha*, joining her for walks in the woods, noting down parts of her lectures from workshops "Soul Mates" into the unique composition of a book, I did my best to answer to this special challenge: to be the best possible medium to a medium.

Spending time with Iris, I have entered a world unknown to me so far, the world of heart vibrations and meditation, searching for light in the hearts of people around me, looking into souls, and not at physical bodies.

All of a sudden I heard and saw deep suffering and uncertain craving for love in the people I mingle with. I stopped taking love for granted, as something which happens or doesn't, which exists or doesn't, which is more or less present, measurable on some continuum of values starting at the imaginary zero. I have accepted that love is something immeasurable, unexplainable and elusive and that every love which happens is a miracle.

Snježana Ivic, Coauthor

About the author

Iris Gattegno Tarbuk has the gift of seeing and communicating with energies and beings in the otherworld an "reading" persons and their souls. She will say she is a soul reader, she can see souls and reads people like books.

In Israel, where she was born, she graduated on the Israeli College for Alternative Medicine and started working especially in the field of counseling people with emotional and psychological problem, using also the Bach flower therapy. During the past thirty years of working on herself, she has further developed her natural talent and today she can recommend people which course to take in order to put in motion their own energy with which they will overcome difficulties and remove blockages.

She has been living in Zagreb since 1995 and has led several workshops titled "Developing intuition" where she taught how to develop attention for the invisible world around us. She has recently developed specific channeled soul mates workshops attended by those who seek true love, but don't succeed in finding their soul mate or their spiritual partner.

She achieved significant results in that field. Attendees of these workshops of guided meditation become aware why they have failed in finding love and learn how to change that. This workshop has gradually become international, with participants from other countries in the region.

Iris was brought by love from Israel to Croatia. She now lives in Zagreb with her husband Branimir, daughter Coral and son Darel, who, she says, taught her what true love is because he sees other people with his heart, sees the soul and not the physical appearance in them.

As an eleven-year-old girl, Iris wrote her wish list. She put helping people to the first place on this list, and she has already realized it. Her second wish was to write a book about how she viewed the world. This book contains only a small part of her spiritual insights she daily channels, but it certainly is the beginning of her childhood wish come true.

In finem

Have you been at Iris?

Iris. Do you know Iris? Have you been at Iris? You must meet Iris!

I have heard this so many times since I met Iris. And it goes a long way. I don't know how long. This confusion with years isn't insignificant, since it seems she had been here before I met her.

Iris is neither psychic, nor a medium. Although on paper she can be all of that, these words sound so indecent when we are talking about Iris. In the world of positive thinking, in the world where everything is measured with acquiring, getting ahead of, competition, in the narrow and small world measured by money, we are lost and disappear in insignificance.

We sever ties with that which unites us, which we are all made from and from where we have all come to stay here for an instant of time, and then return.

The beauty of that wonderful music of love, harmony, joy, compassion, gratitude and modesty, flows through all of us, but we forget it and abandon ourselves to streams of fear which so skillfully shock us, waste our time, separate us from our closest ones, deteriorate our health and shut down our love.

This wonderful woman, our Iris, opens these paths in us like some little God's doorman. Iris touches people and helps us remember that we are all in love perpetually.

When you understand, respect and love Iris, it is as if you understand, respect and love yourself and all the good people around you. And the people around us are always good. We should remember this even when we are taught otherwise.

What is "around us", is something we learn from knowing Iris. My family and me owe her much gratitude. Love is a very simple equation. Everything around us, including ourselves, is love. Iris helps us not to forget it.

Krešimir Dolencic, Theatre Director

www.ingramcontent.com/pod-product-compliance
Lightning Source LLC
LaVergne TN
LVHW011355080426
835511LV00005B/300